Keep 3/09 ED

W9-BCK-840

THE GRAIL

THE GRAIL

THE CELTIC ORIGINS
OF THE SACRED ICON

JEAN MARKALE

TRANSLATED FROM THE FRENCH BY JON GRAHAM

Inner Traditions International
Rochester, Vermont

Inner Traditions International
One Park Street
Rochester, Vermont 05767
www.InnerTraditions.com

First U.S. edition published by Inner Traditions in 1999

Originally published in French in 1982 by Éditions Retz under the title *Le Graal* by
Jean Markale

Library of Congress Cataloging-in-Publication Data

Markale, Jean.
[Graal. English]
The grail : the Celtic origins of the sacred icon / Jean Markale.
p.   cm.
Originally published: Le graal. Paris : Éditions Retz, c1982.
Includes index.
ISBN 0-89281-714-3 (alk. paper)
1. Grail—Romances—History and criticism.   I. Title.
PN686.G7M2813   1999   98-55965
809'.933823—dc21   CIP

Printed and bound in the United States

10 9 8 7 6 5 4 3 2 1

Text design and layout by Virginia L. Scott
This book was typeset in Minion with Mason as the display typeface

Inner Traditions wishes to express its appreciation for assistance given by the
government of France through the ministère de la Culture in the
preparation of this translation.

Nous tenons à exprimer nos plus vifs remerciements au government de la France et le
ministère de la Culture pour leur aide dans le préparation de cette traduction.

Contents

ONE

THE GRAIL OF
CHRÉTIEN DE TROYES

It was between 1180 and 1190 that the Grail made its appearance in
European literature, thanks to the Champagne novelist Chrétien de
Troyes. Chrétien had long been the loyal writer for Eleanor of
Aquitaine's daughter Marie de Champagne and, from what is known,
had a personal relationship with the queen-duchess herself when she
held court at Poitiers. This was a court that welcomed French, Occitan,
Anglo-Norman, and Breton poets and artists, thus constituting an
extraordinary melting pot in which the most diverse cultures and oral
traditions were blended.* It is very likely that the Celtic legends flooded
into French-language literature through Poitiers, where, in passing, they
were colored by all the nuances of Occitan humanism, thereby merging
into the standards of this refined and well-bred society.

No one, before Chrétien de Troyes, had written the name of the Grail.
This doesn't mean to say that the myth of the Grail didn't exist before
him, nor that the word "Grail" was an invention of this writer. But the

---

* See the chapter "The Queen of the Troubadours" in my *Aliénor d'Aquitaine* (Paris:
Payot, 1979), 129–75.

1

facts are as follow: from the chronological perspective, which forms a solid system of reference, Chrétien de Troyes seems to be the initiator of the Grail legend. One can get a clear idea of Chrétien's primary importance through simple consideration of the widespread and enormous fortune his legend has enjoyed. In the end, from the literary standpoint, not a single work dealing with the subject of the Grail can be considered as independent—either wholly or partly—from *Perceval or the Story of the Grail* by Chrétien de Troyes.

Yet, although Chrétien de Troyes's tale seems to be structured on a precise outline, everything is far from clear. The Grail, for those who see it, is quite mysterious. It appears, almost as if by chance, to a wandering hero, a young naïf who doesn't even know his own name, and who definitely doesn't come across as a conqueror. He finds himself in a castle belonging to a wounded king who spends his time fishing from a boat in a lake. Invited to remain at the castle as a guest, the young hero becomes engaged in a trivial conversation with his host, when all at once the atmosphere becomes fantastic.

> While they conversed at their leisure, a page appeared from a neighboring room, holding a sparkling white lance by its handle. He passed between the fire and the couch on which the conversationalists were seated, and all saw the lance and its iron in their whiteness. A drop of blood pearled at the tip of the lance and flowed down its length to the page's hand. Then came two other pages—both quite handsome men—each holding a black-enameled gold chandelier with at least ten burning tapers. Then, following the pages, a beautiful and gentle, nobly adorned damsel appeared, holding a *grail* in her hands. When she entered with the grail such a great light spread through the room that the tapers paled like the stars or moon when the sun rises. The grail was of the purest gold, precious stones were mounted upon it, the most rich and varied that the earth and sea have to offer; no gem can compare to those of the grail. Following the first damsel was another,

who bore a silver tray. Just as the lance had passed before the couch, so did the damsels, who then disappeared into another chamber.*

Thus appears the "Procession of the Grail." The hero, who has been lectured sternly on the subject of discretion by both his mother and the gentleman who knighted him, asks no questions when confronted by this strange spectacle. Later, when he finds himself alone and lost, and the castle has vanished, he learns that if he had asked questions the king would have been healed and his kingdom, now sterile, would have enjoyed great prosperity. This is why the hero, who on the same occasion learns that his name is Perceval, will henceforth devote all his efforts to rediscovering the mysterious castle in order to achieve, in the terms of his quest, the duty he was not able to conclude successfully the first time around.

But Chrétien de Troyes didn't finish his novel. Countless authors following him have taken possession of the grail theme claiming, from their individual perspectives, to supply the true conclusion of Perceval's quest. Now, from all the evidence, the writer from Champagne left behind no outline or rough draft of the ending he intended, if he even intended an ending. All the authors of these continuations have therefore drawn largely from the same sources as Chrétien, in other words Celtic traditions. Their sources, however, have not prevented them from transforming the original myth, which smelled too strongly of paganism, and accentuating the Christian aspect that is already present in *Perceval.* So has the abundant Grail literature been born, in which the Grail has become a sacred vessel containing the blood of Christ.

It will be noted, however, that in Chrétien de Troyes's text, "grail" is a common name. In itself the word is not mysterious: it is derived from the Latin *cratalis,* which is related to the Greek *krater,* through the intermediary of a Languedocian word *cratale.* In modern Occitan it has become *grazala,* "receptacle" or "terrine dish." It should be noted that

---

* Lucien Foulet, trans., *Perceval,* (Paris: Stock, 1947), 75–76.

grazala is a feminine noun, which isn't without significance for interpreting the object. Consequently, the Grail was originally only a *receptacle*, and as such could contain whatever one wished. From the description of the Grail retinue, Chrétien de Troyes strongly refrains from telling us the contents of this object; at the most he insists on the fact that a fantastic light emanated from this receptacle. In any case, Chrétien knowingly maintained the "suspense" as to the Grail's contents. Later, Perceval learns from the gentleman—who is the Fisher King's brother—that the Grail is a "holy thing," and that carried in this Grail is a eucharist that nourishes the wounded king. By this reckoning the Grail is a ciborium and not a chalice. And there is never a mention of the vase containing the blood of Christ gathered by Joseph of Arimathea.

Furthermore, in this procession that has so fired the imaginations of readers and authors, the Grail is not by itself; it is but one of the objects present. There is first of all the Bleeding Lance. The authors of the continuations have transformed this into the lance that the centurion Longinius stabbed into the side of Jesus when he was on the cross, which is a convenient, if excessive interpretation. The Bleeding Lance is, in fact, a well-known folktale element: we are dealing with a weapon that can be used to either kill or heal someone, and which starts to bleed when in the presence of the murderer. This Lance of the Grail can be found in numerous texts that can hardly be suspected of being Christian, namely those of the Irish mythological tradition. Then there is the Silver Tray: in the German adaptation of Chrétien, Wolfram von Eschenbach has made a mistranslation—not the only one, incidentally—by translating the word meaning a plate on which meat is sliced as "knives." In any event the "bloody" nature of the Lance and the Tray is quite evident, a nature that is true to the tone of the original quest, as we will see, for this quest is primarily a story of blood vengeance. In fact, the goal of the original quest is to avenge and heal the mysterious wounded king. In this context, it is not surprising that the authors of the continuations placed the blood of Jesus—crucified to avenge Adam and heal humanity—in the receptacle of the Grail. Even when recuperated by

Christian ideology, the myth retains all its original value.

In any event the Grail procession cannot be separated from Perceval, for whom it becomes both motivation and goal. That is why it is necessary to analyze the story by Chrétien de Troyes, before examining the numerous aspects that have recloaked the legend.

Perceval—who does not yet know his name—is a young man who lives way out in the country with his mother. He is the "Son of the Widowed Lady." His father was wounded in the legs and had remained crippled for a long time before dying. His two brothers were killed in combat. His mother therefore has raised him away from everything, sheltered from the temptations of war, and far removed from the world. The young man spends his time hunting in the forest with spears. One day he meets some knights and is astounded by them, taking them first for devils, then angels, before they explain to him that they are knights of King Arthur. From then on he ceaselessly demands leave of his mother to go to King Arthur and become a knight. Faced with his insistence the Widowed Lady can only let him go, once she has given him instructions that the hero follows to the letter, to his own great inconvenience. He departs the family domain, leaving his mother on the other side of a bridge and, though he sees her swoon, does not retrace his steps.

The entire first part of the book smacks of a traditional tale that can be found at every latitude: the story of a young man, generally poor— here perfectly naive, which is the equivalent—who leaves his parents to seek his fortune. This young man is usually the third son, which is the case here. His two elder brothers have been gone for a long time and have never returned, whether because they have stopped somewhere else along their way or have perished. This third son is apparently the one least likely to profit from his expeditions. And yet it is he who successfully brings the quest to an end. A "Breton lay" written in French at the beginning of the thirteenth century, *The Lay of Tyolet*, presents the same story,* but accentuates the rustic nature of the hero. He is not only a

---

* *Le Coeur Mangé*, erotic and courtly tales presented by Claude Gaigenbet (Paris: Stock-Plus, 1979), 103–20.

skilled hunter, he is also someone who imitates the cries of animals in order to attract them. He is therefore "someone who knows the language of animals," to use the title of another widespread folktale.* This *Lay of Tyolet* enhances our understanding of Perceval's "predestination." He is, in fact, the one who can speak to the animals, the master of the beasts, and as such, he is the shaman who attempts to recreate the primordial times, the Golden Age in which men and beasts lived in understanding of one another, the edenic universe before the fault of Adam. But in the rest of *The Lay of Tyolet* there is no question of a Grail, nor its retinue, nor of some wounded king to be healed.

Chrétien de Troyes scrupulously respected the outline of the traditional folktale. Perceval is truly "John the Sot," a name that is currently utilized for classifying this type of story.† He is happy to highlight, with a remarkable sense of humor, the naiveté and credulity of the young hero. However, at the end of the first part, he adds an element that does not seem gratuitous: when Perceval moves away from the bridge, his mother falls to the ground on the other side and he doesn't go back. This detail will be raised again further on. Chrétien maintains that it is because he is carrying the weight of the sin he committed by allowing his mother to die that Perceval fails the trial of the Grail. This is a rationalizing explanation in the tone of the Christian morality spread by the church, but one that is actually in contradiction with evangelical principles.‡ It was perfectly normal for Perceval to leave his mother and not return; this action corresponds to a rite of passage upon which psychoanalysis has shed some light.

It is true that in his mother's domain, completely isolated and in a

---

* See the Norman version in my *Contes populaires de toute la France* (Paris: Stock, 1980), 185–93.

† See one of the versions of this story, "The Blackbird with the Golden Beak," in my *Contes populaires de toutes les Bretagnes* (Rennes: Ouest-France, 1977), 162–72.

‡ "For I have come to set a man against his father, a daughter against her mother, a daughter-in-law against her mother-in-law. A man's enemies will be those of his own household" (Matthew 10:35). "That is why a man must leave his father and mother, and become one with his wife" (Mark 10:7).

somewhat savage state, Perceval was in the uterine universe in an undifferentiated and, in some respects, *unborn* state. This, moreover, justifies the bisexual aspect that many authors gave to the Grail hero.* It is therefore indispensable that he *burn his bridges* to his previous state in order to be born, hence the scene at the bridge. The scene with his mother, in other words the action with which he cuts his own umbilical cord, is tragic only because it takes place too late. Perceval should have been more severe at a much earlier date, but his mother (the image of the devouring, phallic mother) could not support such a rupture since it would mean that her son was making his definitive escape from her, thus destroying her reason to live. But from another angle, by virtue of the fact that he was nourished for too long on maternal milk, at least symbolically, Perceval has acquired a superhuman strength that allows him to overcome obstacles no matter how insurmountable. We recognize here another widespread folktale that concerns a child who is overendowed because he was weaned too late.[†]

At this point we find our hero on the path to his maturity. He still has much to do. Astonished, not to say stupefied, by what he sees, and recalling the advice of his mother, which he stupidly interprets literally, he steals a ring, a meat pie, and a kiss from a young damsel. After journeying on without incident he reaches the court of King Arthur. There he shamelessly rides his horse into the room where Arthur is holding court surrounded by his knights. He has arrived at an inopportune moment. The king has just been subjected to the scorn of an unknown knight who stole his cup and spilled its contents all over Queen Guinivere, and then left again giving challenge to all the knights. The queen had retired to her room "where she was dying of rage and sorrow." Perceval, with a

---

* In his *Parzival*, the German director Syberberg, who filmed Wagner's opera of the same name (1982), had the role of Parzifal played by both a young man and a young woman.
* See in particular "Rannou le Frot et Yanning au bâton de fer" in my book *La Tradition celtique en Bretagne armoricaine*, 3rd ed. (Paris: Payot, 1978), 140–42 and 224–29, as well as "Les aventures de Yann Baz-Houarn" in my *Contes populaires de toutes les Bretagne*, 157–61. In this last tale, the hero remains in his mother's belly for three years, from which he acquires a formidable strength.

naiveté that borders on the unconscious, kills the criminal knight with a lance, returns the cup to the queen, promises to avenge himself on the seneschal Kay who had made fun of him, takes possession of the arms and armor of his victim, and leaves, renouncing, for the moment, his desire to be dubbed a knight by King Arthur, whom he deems to have an overrated reputation.

The damsel from whom he stole the ring, the meat pie, and the kiss is obviously the symbolic image of the outside world of which the hero is ignorant. She is also his first contact with femininity, which has resulted in a failure, as he has not won her heart. His desire to be knighted has led him to disillusionment; this implies that he is not destined to membership in an earthly knighthood, *like the others*, which doesn't prevent him from vanquishing the criminal knight. It will be noted that the cup whose contents were spilt upon Queen Guinivere, a cup that Perceval recovers with no great difficulty, prefigures the Grail. But, in any case— if using Chrétien de Troyes's text as a guide—the hero is not conscious of his actions. As for the fact that he enters the king's chamber on horseback, even if Chrétien used it as a manifestation of Perceval's naiveté, this is a reference to an ancient Celtic model. In fact the first Celtic fortresses consisted of a certain number of single-story houses grouped in a fortified camp.* This is a detail that hardly conforms with the general atmosphere of Chrétien's romance, that of the civilization of the end of the twelfth century, with its solid castle-forts in stone, but does, on the other hand, testify to the antiquity of the model that the writer used.

Meanwhile Perceval wanders through the forest, quite irritated with the horse that he doesn't know how to mount and the weapons that he doesn't know how to use. He finds shelter at the castle of a gentleman, Gornemant de Goort, who teaches him how to ride a horse, to wield a

---

* Good examples of Celtic fortresses can be seen at Maiden Castle, near Dorchester, in England, at the Camp d'Artus in Huelgoat (Finistère), and in Alaise (the Jura region), which is probably the actual site of Alésia. See J. Markale, *Vercingétorix* (Paris: Hachette, 1982), 218–29.

lance and a sword, and then knights him after having lavished him with advice complementary to that of his mother. Perceval is then received in another castle by the beautiful Blanchefleur. He is mistaken for a mute at first because he doesn't speak, thus putting into practice the advice of his mother and Gornemant. But he eventually answers the questions asked of him. That night the beautiful Blanchefleur comes to him in his room, wearing somewhat inappropriate attire, and requests his aid in ridding her of the enemies who seek to drive her from her domains. Perceval, still applying his mother's counsel, which dictates that he must always help a lady or a maiden, promises that he will fight for her. And that night the beautiful Blanchefleur shares his bed.

It is obvious that Perceval cannot wander long in a state of almost total ignorance. This is why Chrétien de Troyes has him meet Gornemant. All the folktales contrive the meeting of the young man with an old man or woman who will inform him of his destiny in one manner or another. This is perhaps the description of a secret initiator or "guru" who has a stake in directing a zealous young man toward an objective about which he has inside knowledge. From this moment, Perceval has ascended several rungs: he has passed from the domain of the unconscious to the subconscious. And his conduct and acceptance at Blanchefleur's castle proves it. The various commentators on the Grail legend, who are barely familiar with any but the German text of Wolfram von Eschenbach, have long expounded on the chastity necessary for the hero to become king of the Grail. It is true that the continuators of Chrétien, by dint of Christianizing the legend, could only accentuate Perceval's chaste aspect by suppressing, as much as possible, those details that were morally shocking. But in the version of the writer from Champagne, as in the Welsh tale of *Peredur*, which seems to be the folk version of the legend, there is absolutely no consideration of Perceval's virginity or chastity. Chrétien's tale is quite clear. When Perceval accepts the job of fighting for Blanchefleur, the latter—who had come in the middle of the night, flimsily attired, in order to wrest the young man's consent—slid into her guest's bed at his invitation. "The maiden suffered his kisses and I do not believe it was at great cost for her. Thus they spent the night together side by side, mouth to mouth, until the morning and the approach of day." In brief, Perceval receives his sexual initiation from Blanchefleur after receiving his warrior's initiation from Gornemant de Goort. This second initiation also conforms to the standard folktale outline. There are countless examples in the folk literature of quests in which the young hero—weak or callow, but good and generous—loses his innocence at the hands of mysterious women scattered throughout his journey. These commonly appear as multifarious witches or beautiful, young fairies, and even as women who resemble Saint Anne or the Holy Virgin.* Whether or not sexual relations take place between the hero and the initiating woman, the result is identical: the hero traverses a decisive stage of his quest, attains a greater maturity that brings to nothing his earlier delusions that were an obstacle to his blossoming, and receives indications—sometimes coded—concerning the path he must follow.

But it is probable that in the archetype of Chrétien's Perceval, whatever his immediate model was, it was the same person who dispensed the warrior's sexual initiation, and this person could only have been Blanchefleur. There is still a trace of this in the Welsh *Peredur*—the archaic and folk version of the legend—where the hero departs to be initiated by the "witches of Caer Lloyw." Here we find ourselves completely immersed in ancient Celtic tradition. Mythological Irish tales are full of examples of this sort, and two tales in particular are quite revelatory in this regard. These are *The Education of Cuchulainn*, the remaining version of which is found in a sixteenth-century manuscript but whose details are quite archaic, and *The Courtship of Emer*, an eleventh-century manuscript that deals with the same subject in a more restrained fashion. Analysis of the roots of these texts brings to light a very primitive society, governed by customs Christianity hadn't completely succeeded in abolishing, and whose memory is still quite vital. In

* See in particular "The Women-swans" and "The Land of the Fairies" in my *La tradition celtique*, 186, 192; "The Young Girl in White" and "The Three Dogs" in my *Contes populaires de toutes les Bretagne*, 36, 245; and my *Contes occitans* (Paris: Stock, 1981), 223.

these texts we learn that there were women-warriors who taught the young members of the nobility, and that certain persons among these women bear names that are quite thought-provoking: Scatach (she who causes fear) and Uatach (the very terrible one). There is a great temptation to say that we are dealing here with "druidesses." But we have no real proof for the existence of so-called druidesses. On the other hand we know, through certain bits of testimony, that some women belonged to the druidic class, generally as prophets or poets. It would be possible to rank these women-warriors with the witchlike aspects associated with a lower category of druids. This is quite plausible as the Celts, unlike the Greeks and Romans who have male warrior gods, have a female deity holding the warrior function. We don't know her Gallic name but she was called Bodbh or Morrigan by the Irish. Bodbh means "crow." It is precisely in the form of a crow that Bodbh-Morrigan often appears in the epic sagas, just like the Morgana of the Round Table stories, who is the fairy-sorceress-warrior revised and corrected by the medieval mentality. The name Bodbh can also be connected to the Gallic name *bodo* or *bodu* that not only means "crow" but "victory" as well. This gives reason to believe that many of the mounds and mountains placed under the name of Saint Victoire were formerly sites of worship consecrated to an ancient goddess of war.

The women-warriors who taught the young hero Cuchulainn were clearly sorceresses. They taught him skills that smack as much of the magical arts as they do of military arts. Moreover, they liberally bestowed upon the hero—according to the time-honored phrase—the "friendship of their thighs." Incidentally, the origin of all the fabrications that the Christian West used to start the "witch hunts," accusing the "witches" of fornication as well as malefic acts, can be seen in these traces of an ancient society. In any case it was thanks to these women-warriors that Cuchulainn become almost invincible.* Finn, another Irish hero, also acquired his formidable, magical-warrior powers from

---

* Jean Markale, *L Épopée celtique d'Irlande*, 2nd ed. (Paris: Payot, 1978), 88–95.

warrior women who took him in following the death of his parents.* With this background information why contest the role Blanchefleur would have played in the original version of the Quest, a role now split in two by reason of its transposition into a social system that no longer recognized that the roles of woman and warrior could be united in one person, a double function inherited from the dawn of time?

Accordingly, on the next day Perceval engages the enemies of Blanchefleur, Clamadou and his seneschal Aguingueron, in combat. He defeats them and sends them as prisoners to Arthur's court, profiting from the occasion to warn Kay that he will get his revenge on him. He remains for a while longer with Blanchefleur but is haunted by the image of his mother. Eventually, unaware that she has died, he leaves to rejoin her.

Perceval has therefore attained maturity as a warrior. He is, in some respects, invincible. Sated with victory and love, it is possible to believe that he is "going on retreat." A traditional folktale would end here. But Perceval's drama is that he is *falsely born:* his attachment to his mother is still too strong even if he is subconsciously convinced that she is dead. He wants reassurance in one form or another, hence his departure. But he has no idea of where he is or how to find his way back to his mother's domain. Perceval is totally lost in a world that, if not hostile, is at least unknown and foreign. This explains Perceval's errantry, which is of a different nature than the errantry of the other Arthurian knights. An Arthurian knight would leave Arthur's court in search of great deeds to accomplish and on a predetermined day would return to the court in order to recount his adventures to the other knights. It is each knight's individual prowess that honors and enlarges the community formed by the Knights of the Round Table. It is true that each time Perceval vanquishes an adversary he sends him prisoner to King Arthur's court in apparent respect to this rule: the prisoner of one individual is the prisoner of the community. But Perceval was not seeking prowess, *he was in search of himself,* for at bottom he had no idea who he was. Furthermore

* Ibid., 141–49.

he didn't even know his own name, which is very revealing of his interior errantry. Until then he was only the "Son of the Widowed Lady," a simple "Welsh valet" (since the only reference to his origins concerns the country of Wales). This misrecognition of himself fully justifies both his desire to find his mother again and the incoherent nature of his itinerary.

This is the point at which Perceval meets the mysterious fisherman who invites him to spend the night at his castle. He sees that both his host's legs are crippled. A valet brings the Fisher King a sword that was "of a steel so hard that it couldn't be broken save by one danger alone, known only to he who had forged and tempered it." The king gives this sword to Perceval who doesn't find any cause for surprise in this action. Then the famous Grail procession appears. Perceval, out of discretion, asks no questions. After a hearty meal he is ushered into a chamber where he sleeps the sleep of the just. The next morning the castle is completely empty. Despite Perceval's frantic search he cannot find a living soul. He leaves the castle and the drawbridges are raised behind him. Once more Perceval finds himself in the forest in a state of complete disorder.

It is obvious that the Fisher King's wound is reminiscent of the wound of Perceval's own father, emphasized by the fact that there are bonds of kinship between the two men. The Fisher King is—although the hero doesn't know this yet—his uncle, or his cousin, the text isn't very clear on this point. In any event when Perceval finds himself at the Grail Castle he also finds himself at home with his family, with his "clan." This is the reason he is given the sword that is destined to be broken in a predetermined situation. We are in the presence of one of those magic or holy swords with which epic literature is so rich. It brings to mind Excalibur ("hard cutting" in Welsh), the magic sword of Arthur that corresponds to the Irish Caladbolg, the sword of the god Nuada of the Silver Hand that "no one could escape when drawn from its warrior's scabbard and which no one could withstand."* In addition it

---

* George Dottin, *L'Épopée irlandaise*, new ed. presented by J. Markale (Paris: Les Presses d'Aujourd'hui, 1980), 17.

would burn the hand of anyone who took hold of it without just cause. It is also reminiscent of Durandal, Siegfried's sword, and, of course, the Sword of the Strange Belt that plays such an important role in later tales of the Quest.

Perceval was therefore recognized as someone who must perform a mission, by all the evidence one that would verge on being a bellicose and bloody act. He must perform an action with the sword, but just what that action will be remains unknown, and before undertaking the action Perceval must undergo another test, that of the Grail. He does not succeed because he is not yet himself, because he has not yet attained the necessary maturity. He is not driven from the castle but flees from it: driven to desperation by his solitude, he can only resume his errantry. Now, more than ever, Perceval is lost.

He encounters a young girl mourning over the decapitated body of her lover. This young girl reveals certain elements of Perceval's quest to him. She informs him that she is his cousin. She tells him his name: Perceval the Welshman. She tells him that if he had asked the questions "What is the Grail and who does it serve?" he would have healed the Fisher King and restored prosperity to his kingdom. And, according to her, Perceval's failure is the result of his sin, because he has caused "his mother to die of sorrow." Finally she warns him that his sword will break treacherously and that if he wishes to repair it he must go to the "Lake of Cotoatre," to the home of the "smith Trébuchet," for "he is the man who made and will remake the sword or else it will never be reforged by anyone."

How far we are from Wagner and the triumph of Parzival, king of the Grail! It is true that it was the authors of the continuations, Wolfram von Eschenbach in particular, who invented the myth of the royalty of the Grail. This Grail royalty appears to be totally absent from Chrétien de Troyes's text. It proves that even if he had completed his work, this author would never have made Perceval into a king of the Grail. The goal of his quest was quite different and it is discernible with the aid of the three most ancient Grail texts, to wit the Welsh *Peredur*, the Occitan romance of *Jauffré*, and the strange Anglo-Norman tale of *Perlesvaus*, which we will speak of in detail later. The key to the problem is the sword: in the original outline used by Chrétien de Troyes, the Grail is only an episode, an initiatory test of character certainly, but simply one stage. The goal is completely different: it concerns blood vengeance. This observation is of capital importance for the understanding of the myth of the Grail and its ensuing transformations. And it is proof that the tale by de Troyes remains quite close to an entirely pagan archetype that can be recognized in various convergent texts of indisputably Celtic origin.

Perceval continues to wander. He doesn't know where he is going. He encounters the young girl from whom he had stolen the pie, ring, and kiss, acts for which she has been mistreated by her companion. They reconcile. Finally he finds himself on a plain close to the place where Arthur holds his court. It has been snowing since the night before and a goose wounded by a falcon loses three drops of blood upon the snow, whereupon Perceval falls into an ecstatic trance because these drops on the snow

> remind him of the vivid colors of Blanchefleur, his lover. He aban-
> doned himself so readily to thoughts of her that he forgot where he
> was. As the vermilion sprung forth on the whiteness of his lover's
> face so did the three drops of blood detach themselves from the
> whiteness of the snow. (Foulet trans., 78)

Chrétien de Troyes has received much praise for the delicate handling of this episode and some have even sought a symbolic meaning for it in connection with the blood of Christ. However, truth obliges me to say that Chrétien's authorship is negligible because this episode, delicate imagery included, is unquestionably an archetype. In fact, the Welsh version of *Peredur* portrays the same scene:

> Snow had fallen during the night and a falcon had killed a duck. A
> raven was tearing at the flesh of the bird. Peredur stood there, com-
> paring the blackness of the bird and whiteness of the snow and red-
> ness of the blood to the appearance of the woman he loved best:

> her hair was black as jet, her skin was white as snow and the two
> red spots in her cheeks like the blood in the snow.*

The poetry is even more intense in the Welsh text. But for those who claim that *Peredur* is an adaptation of Chrétien's tale, it should be added that the same image can be found in a much earlier Irish tale, *The Story of Deirdre*. The young Deirdre witnesses a servant skinning a calf on the snow and a raven alighting to drink its blood. Then Deirdre says: "The sole man I will love will be he who has these three colors, hair like the raven, cheeks like blood, and skin like snow" (Dottin, *LÉpopée irlandaise*, 66).

In short, it is quite clearly a question of a cliché from Celtic amorous literature. Furthermore, it will be noted that Chrétien de Troyes has slightly modified the original model: in fact, as he had previously described Blanchefleur as having hair that could be mistaken "to be gold, so lustrous and sparkling it was," it was certainly necessary for him to omit the raven. In any event, this provides proof that Chrétien followed a model of Celtic origin, which he turned to his advantage with rare good fortune, and adapted to his personal tastes.

Meanwhile, King Arthur has spied Perceval standing immobile in the snow and sends several of his knights to invite him over. But Perceval, completely lost in a trance, contents himself with knocking each of the knights over, one after the other, particularly Kay, thus unconsciously achieving the vengeance he had promised the seneschal. Then for the sake of peace Arthur sends Gawain. Through his wise words this latter individual persuades Perceval to come into the presence of the king. The hero is honored as he deserves.

It is in this fashion that Gawain makes his entrance into Perceval's quest. His invasion of the tale is not arbitrary and, in addition, it presents a typically Celtic feature. Indeed, in all the Welsh texts, Gwalchmai (the Welsh name of Gawain), Arthur's favorite nephew—from the maternal side, of course—is the man for delicate situations, diplomatic

* Joseph Loth, trans., *Les Mabinogion*, vol. 2 (Paris: Fontemoing, 1913), 76.

endeavors, and reconciliations. When, in the short Welsh tale *The Story of Tristan*, King Mark demands King Arthur's intervention on his behalf in his dispute with Tristan, it is Gawain-Gwalchmai who succeeds in calming Tristan's murderous rage and bringing him to Arthur. In this text Gawain-Gwalchmai is even given the title "chief of peace."* It is apparent that he plays the same role in Chrétien's *Perceval*. From this moment on Arthur's nephew plays an important part in the quest, to such an extent that it could be rightfully asked if he wasn't the original hero of this story.

Perceval remains at Arthur's court. One has the impression that he has completely forgotten Blanchefleur, the Grail castle, and the death of his mother. Then one day a young girl arrives, mounted on a mule. But what a young girl! She is horrible. Chrétien takes advantage of her awful appearance to tell us he is giving her description according to the book, which leads us to believe that he was using a written source for *Perceval*.

> Never was metal seen as gray as her cheeks and even more her hands. Her eyes were simple pits, no bigger than those of a rat, her nose was of a cat or a monkey, her lips were like those of an ass or an ox, her teeth were as yellow as egg yolk, they were so orange and she had a beard like a billy-goat. A hump protruded from the center of her chest, her spine seemed crooked, she had the waist and shoulders of a well-built man, perfect for leading the ball, a hump on her back and twisted legs like willow wands: well was she made to lead the dance! (Foulet trans.)

This savory description could be credited to a novelist wishing to amuse his readers. It is nothing of the sort. This hideously ugly woman can be found in numerous Irish mythological tales. In truth she is a character from folklore. It frequently occurs that a young hero, like Perceval, will come across a woman equally ugly during the course of his journey. It is then necessary for him to undergo a test: if he flees in fear

* Jean Markale, *L'Épopée celtique en Bretagne*, 2nd ed. (Paris: Payot, 1975), 221.

or mocks the woman he foredooms his quest to failure. For this hideous woman holds the fate of the hero in her hands. If the hero takes pity on her, and deals with her generously, she will reward him by telling him what he should do or by giving him a magic object. Wolfram von Eschenbach wasn't fooled: he made this hideous maiden on the mule the disturbing Cundrie the Sorceress. For this woman is truly a witch, that is to say a supernatural character, a sorceress, or a fairy. She has numerous guises and appears next in the form of a young girl of rare beauty. The test imposed upon the hero therefore consists of allowing him to master his repugnance. Often, this woman demands that those she meets give her a kiss. The majority refuse, but there is always one who overcomes his disgust: then the old and horrible woman transforms into a ravishing young girl who either offers the hero youth, amorous prowess, treasure, or sovereignty.

For Chrétien de Troyes, the "hideous Maiden on the Mule," like Cundrie for Wolfram, is the messenger of the Grail. In the Welsh *Peredur* she is the Empress, indicative of her power. Whatever name she appears under, she originates in an ancient epic from the Ulster cycle. There she is the character of Leborcham, an ugly, deformed woman, who is the messenger for Conchobar, king of the Ulaid. But note: "Leborcham could not be attacked for she was a witch" (Dottin, *L'Épopée irlandaise*, 66). There is nothing gratuitous about the repulsive aspect attributed to witches during the Middle Ages. A witch who has certain powers at her disposal—for ill as well as good—is obliged to hide her true personality, without which her powers would become common property. By hiding her powers she hides her beauty under a hideous surface in order to discourage those who only pay heed to appearances. In fact, "the door is on the inside." It requires only eyes to see and ears to hear. It is only at the moment when Oedipus can answer the Sphinx's question (in reality a female entity) that he can understand femininity. Before he saw her under the monstrous form of the phallic and devouring mother, since the sphinx was none other than Oedipus's mother. Henceforth he saw her under the aspect of Jocasta. Unfortunately the gods—the projection of society and its norms—banded together against this incestuous union. All of this implies that Perceval's spirit awakens completely with the appearance of "the hideous Maiden on the Mule."

This messenger insults Perceval for not having asked questions during his stay at the Grail castle. Because of this missed opportunity "women will lose their husbands, the lands will be devastated, the maidens without support will become orphans and many knights will die." This is obviously not a question regarding the royalty of the Grail. It is simply a regenerative act that Perceval can achieve.

However, the "hideous Maiden on the Mule" is a messenger. She has come to reveal a possible way out of this dilemma. She declares that at the peak of a hill, in the castle of Montesclaire, a young girl is being held prisoner. The knight that frees her will acquire a supreme honor from that deed. Better yet, he will be able to gird on "the sword of the strange belt" without fear. But to succeed, he must go before Castle Orguelleus and boldly fight the noble knights there.

It will be noted that the messenger remains mute concerning the location of the castle of the Grail. The direction she indicates is completely different. We are now dealing with the deliverance of a mysterious "maiden." And the victor will be able to gird on the no less mysterious "sword of the strange belt," in other words, another weapon with which he will be able to perform a bloody deed.

In a fine display of unanimity those knights present declare that they will hasten before Castle Orguelleus. Gawain shouts the loudest and Chrétien de Troyes shows himself most inclined to follow his quest from this point forward. As for Perceval, he effectively bestirs himself from his torpor but not to follow the others' lead. Indeed he vows that he will not spend two consecutive nights in the same place "until the day he finally knows who is served by the Grail and where the bleeding lance can be found, and learns, beyond the shadow of a doubt, why it is bleeding" (Foulet trans., 112).

In short, Perceval ignores Castle Orguelleus. The messenger's intervention has revived his memories and he departs in search of the Grail while Gawain goes in search of the damsel to be delivered. This is not the first time that Chrétien de Troyes utilizes the double quest outline.

Previously, in his *Knight of the Cart*, he portrayed Gawain and Lancelot of the Lake leaving to free Queen Guinivere by two different roads. Lancelot entered the kingdom of Gorre (or Verre), in other words, a land in the Otherworld ruled by the god Meleagant, by way of the "Bridge of the Sword." Here he had to cross a raging river spanned by a sharp sword. But Gawain had entered the same kingdom by the "Bridge under the Water," and it is he, incidentally, who earns the honor of delivering the queen. These two bridges are strangely reminiscent of the two alchemical methods that allow one to achieve the Great Work (these are the dry path called the short path and the wet path known as the long path), that is to say they represent the Philosopher's Stone. Aside from this reference one cannot fail to be struck by the ambiguous nature of the Quest as seen by Chrétien de Troyes.

It is in fact, despite the imbalance between them, one and the same quest that takes Gawain to Montesclaire and Perceval toward the castle of the Grail. The path of Gawain, the moist path without a doubt, since, as we will see, he passes by a fisherman, is suited to his personality. Gawain is skillful, courteous, diplomatic, courageous, true to his word *except in love:* he is a natural born heartbreaker and is unable to resist a woman when the occasion presents itself. Thus it is normal that his quest would entail the deliverance of the mysterious maiden, for until then, he has loved women but not the one woman destined for him. Perceval, to the contrary, has discovered Blanchefleur and is unable to forget her: she is the unique, beloved woman. Perceval's path is therefore the dry path. He hurls himself into this quest for the Grail with his head down in utter unconsciousness. But he still doesn't know which direction he should take.

Chrétien de Troyes then good-naturedly describes Gawain's numerous adventures. Arthur's nephew has imprudently promised his aid to an "evil maid" whose presence particularly weakens him. With somewhat diabolical overtones, this evil maid constantly enmeshes him in unlooked-for adventures, causing him to stray farther and farther from his path. As for Perceval, he wanders for five years fighting the knights he meets, whom he then sends prisoner to Arthur's court.

One Holy Friday, however, Perceval finds himself reproached by knights and ladies who urge him to perform penance for being armed on that day. Perceval heeds their counsel and finds a saintly hermit who is none other than his uncle. His uncle reproaches him for the sin he committed by causing his mother's death, provides him several revelations about the Grail, "an object so holy," and particularly about another wounded king, the father of the Fisher King, who remains cloistered in the chamber in which Perceval had seen the Grail disappear. The hermit urges Perceval to cleanse himself of his sins and henceforth live a Christian life. Perceval remains ten days in the company of his uncle who "spoke an orison in his ear and repeated it until he knew it. Many names of God were included, among them the greatest which the mouth of man should never utter save for in fear of death. He also forbid him from saying it in any way without great peril" (Foulet trans., 153). Perceval takes leave of the hermit on the day of Easter, and the author says nothing more of his title character in the rest of the book.

Indeed, the following part of the work concerns the numerous adventures of Gawain alone. These adventures of Arthur's nephew are complicated and seemingly lifted unchanged from related secondary tales. Indeed the hero is subsequently seen in a Revolving Castle tormented by devils, then he is received by a mysterious "Queen with white tresses," who is none other than Ygerne, Arthur's mother and Gawain's own grandmother. Chrétien takes this occasion to insert some strange words concerning Queen Guinivere: "Since the first woman was formed from Adam's rib there has not been a woman of such renown. . . . My lady the queen instructs and teaches all those alive. From her descends all the good of the world, she is its source and origin." You have to wonder if you are dreaming: here in the middle of the twelfth century, an era of triumphant Christianity, it is not the Virgin Mary (whose worship was widespread as is well known) upon whom Gawain bestows his praise— while at the same time submitting himself to the Perfect Being—but the adulterous wife of King Arthur who clearly appears here to be wearing one of the faces of the ancient Mother Goddess of the Celts.

Meanwhile, through a complex series of enchantments and adventures,

Gawain finds himself prisoner in Ygerne's castle. He sends a messenger to King Arthur to compel the latter to come, and the messenger acquits himself of his mission most favorably. But here the tale is interrupted: Chrétien de Troyes didn't take it any further and we will never know what he imagined to be the contents of that mysterious receptacle, the Holy Grail. This is the point at which the authors of countless continuations have picked up the thread of the story and extended it in every possible direction.

TWO⊙

The
Franco-British Grail

The Welsh Tale of Peredur

The Welsh tale of Peredur is contained within two different medieval manuscripts. One is known under the name of *The Red Book of Hergest*, dating from the fourteenth century. The other, which is actually a collection of different manuscripts, is called the *White Book of Rydderch*. The part containing *Peredur* dates from the beginning of the thirteenth century. But the age of the manuscripts proves nothing. Taking the details and French—or Norman to be precise—influence into account, an influence that is undeniable and to be expected for the Wales of this era, *Peredur*'s composition can be pushed back to the end of the twelfth century. However, despite what some maintained earlier this century, *Peredur* is in no way an adaptation of Chrétien de Troyes's *Perceval*, much less a translation. Careful study of the two texts—which has been done on many occasions—ends with the conclusion that was originally put forth by Joseph Loth, the first French translator of *Peredur* in 1913, that both the author of *Peredur* and Chrétien de Troyes used a written French source text that was a translation or adaptation of a text that was originally Welsh or Armorican-Breton. Chrétien de Troyes made his tale courtly by going along with the dictates of then contemporary aristocratic French style, glossing over the coarseness of the story, and trying to make the incredible adventures he recounted seem plausible. In contrast, the version by the Welsh author, even though he was influenced by Norman civilization, retains a certain uncouth air, a succession of seemingly incoherent events, a Celtic mentality, and certain archaic details that testify to an outline dating quite far back.

The hero is named Peredur. The Welsh word *peir*, meaning "cauldron," has been seen by some in the first syllable of this name, which is very tempting since Peredur will find himself in the presence of the famous Celtic cauldron of abundance and resurrection that is one of the Grail's prototypes. But this seems quite improbable: Peredur was quite a common masculine name in medieval Wales. The question to be asked is whether or not the archetypal text contains this name, which is something we don't know. There is even a kinship between the name Perceval and Peredur if only by the first syllable. The anonymous author of *Perlesvaus* creates a curious etymology and provides justification for it in his story. The name of the hero, Perlesvaus in this instance would be in fact Perd les Vaux (Lose the Valley). By this reckoning Perceval would be the Picardy form of Perd le Val: Perd ce Val. Parzifal (or Parsifal) is merely the German transcription of this name. It has been noted that Chrétien de Troyes named his hero Perceval *the Welshman*. Was this because he knew the archetype was in the Welsh language? In the Welsh tale, Peredur is called ab Efrawg, "son of Evroc." It so happens that Evroc is the Welsh name for York (Caer Efrawg), which allows one to assume that Peredur was considered as the son of the Count of York. Consequently he wouldn't be Welsh, unless the original outline for the story goes back to the time before the Saxons occupied England and York was located, like the regions of the future land of Wales, in the same insular Britain. In any event, there can be no doubt as to the Britannic origin—that is to say belonging to the group of insular Britons and Armorican Bretons—of Peredur-Perceval's quest.

Count Efrawg had seven sons but because he was such an impassioned amateur at tournaments he was killed, as were six of his sons. The seventh was Peredur who is immediately named in the tale. Peredur was raised by his mother in a remote location, far removed from the world and its fuss, and especially from anything smacking of knights and chivalry. The young boy was fourteen years old and everyday would go into the forest to throw and play with darts and staffs" (Loth, II, 48).

Peredur is the preeminent wild child. He is even more uncouth than the youth portrayed in Chrétien's story, but it is not said that he knows the speech of animals as in *Tyolet*. He is presented as a naïf—at best—and in a curious passage he herds goats and deer together believing that the latter are goats who have lost their horns. It should be noted that the author's reference to tournaments, something totally unknown in Welsh custom, would appear to be a concession to Norman fashions.

One day, as in Chrétien's book, Peredur meets three knights, Gwalchmai (Gawain), Gweir, and Owein (Yvain) in pursuit of a foe. Peredur at first mistakes them for angels: this is at least the claim of his mother who doesn't wish to say the word "knights." Peredur engages them in conversation, and instead of answering their questions, he makes them explain what knights are. He then wishes to depart straight away for Arthur's court in order to become a knight. To his mother's great sorrow he decides to leave. But she bestows some pieces of advice upon him:

> When you see a church, recite your paternoster. Wherever you see food and drink and you have need of them, and they are not offered to you out of goodwill and courtesy, then take them. If you hear cries, go there, especially if it is the cry of a woman. If you see fine pieces of jewelry, take them and give them to another, and you will earn a good reputation. If you see a beautiful woman, woo her, even if she does not wish it, for she will deem you better and more powerful than before. (Loth trans., vol. 2, 51–52)

The least that can be said is that this is strange advice. There is a tangible difference between it and that given Perceval by his mother, but even more odd is that Chrétien's Perceval follows the advice given Peredur to the letter. This is more proof of the existence of a common source text used by the two authors, although Chrétien seems not to have understood his model very well at this juncture. In any case, and whatever its origin may have been, Wolfram's German text contains an element found neither in Peredur nor Perceval. This is another piece of advice given Parzival that counsels him to avenge himself on the proud Lähelin who has taken possession of his father's states and killed his principal vassals. The theme of blood vengeance, implied by Chrétien de Troyes, mainly with the episode of the sword, and made perfectly explicit at the end of *Peredur*, is evoked again here. Moreover the name of Lähelin seems to stem from the Germanic *hell*, meaning the infernal regions or the goddess of hell, which has clear ties to witches. We will see that Peredur's vengeance must be enacted against witches.

Armed with some wooden spears, Peredur leaves without a backward glance. There is no mention of a bridge or the death of his mother here. He wanders through the woods. Arriving near a pavilion, he thinks that it is a church and recites his paternoster. He then enters the pavilion and finds a young woman there who gives him a warm welcome. He avidly eats and drinks what he finds there and demands that the maiden give him her ring. She gives it to him with good heart and Perceval takes his leave. But the young woman's companion takes it badly and promises to seek his revenge on Peredur.

It is apparent that this tale, in its main lines, is quite close to *Perceval*. However, there are varying nuances in the detail. The naiveté of the hero is less morbid: it would seem that Peredur was a being who had determined to follow the train of his thought through to the bitter end and scorned reality. As for the young woman in the pavilion, she may well have been one of the numerous feminine—and fairylike—apparitions that mark out Peredur's quest. In any event she *gives* him her ring, a gesture that prefigures a later episode. It provides a better comprehension of the corresponding episode in Chrétien's work, in which Perceval symbolically loses his virginity by taking the young girl's ring by force. The image of the ring is quite eloquent and it is well known that the wedding band passed over the finger of the bride announces the consummation of the marriage by the penetration of the penis in the vagina. But if Perceval, by taking the ring, committed a rape, Peredur had before him a veritable initiator who made him a gift of her sex.

Without further delay, like all "sad animals" *post coïtum*, Peredur leaves and makes his way to Arthur's court. Before his arrival a knight had presented himself before Arthur, taken possession of Gwenhwyvar's (Guinivere's) cup, dashed its contents in her face, and taken his leave while challenging the knights present to meet him in single combat in the field facing the castle.

There are differences with Chrétien's tale here that are important. With Chrétien it is the king's cup that is stolen, though its contents are spilled upon the queen. With the Welsh author it's Gwenhwyvar's cup and the outrage is entirely directed against the queen. A supplementary detail in Wolfram's text allows us to get a better understanding: the intruder is in fact the Red Knight, Arthur's cousin, who has come to reclaim his birthright.

Thus this scene is made clearer, especially in the Welsh version where it assumes its full significance. The cup obviously prefigures the Grail, and the intruder's provocative gesture will actually launch Peredur into the Grail Quest, since his first deed is the recovery of the cup. On the other hand, the Grail, portrayed as a simple plate in the Welsh version, is a bisexual object. Indeed, and people have not failed to remark upon this on numerous occasions, the Grail, when described as a cup or a receptacle, is a feminine symbol, all the more so as it is carried by a young girl, in Chrétien's version the Fisher King's daughter. Here it is a question of Gwenhwyvar's cup. Don't forget that the word *grazala* in Occitan is feminine. But it is the cup itself, the *container,* that is feminine; what it holds, the *contents,* can only be masculine whether it is wine (as in this scene) or blood (as in the majority of versions). When one refers to the Last Supper in which Jesus performed the transubstantiation of wine into his own blood, the identical nature of the two substances cannot be doubted, anyway. No matter which substance the container holds, it is still a symbol, a substitution. We are in fact dealing with the sperm held in the vagina after coitus. And the gesture of over-turning the cup on the queen reinforces this interpretation. In reality the intruder has simply raped the queen.

But this rape is complex. For as the quintessential embodiment of sovereignty Gwenhwyvar has been struck in her very essence. The offending knight has committed a political crime and baffled legitimate authority. Moreover, according to Wolfram, he has come to reclaim his birthright, which assumes he casts doubt on the power held by Arthur in Gwenhwyvar's name. On the social plane the queen represents the entire community for which she is the mother, sister, wife, and lover. This rape, a transgression of the fundamental ban on incest, concerns every member of the community. On the spiritual level, grouping reli-gion and morality together, it is a sacrilege, given the sacred nature of the queen. In a text that comes later than Chrétien's *Perceval* but which claims to precede it, *The Elucidation*, we are told that the Grail has dis-appeared in consequence of a rape committed by the king on one of the fairy guardians of the sacred vessel. It is certain that in this episode from *Peredur* (and *Perceval*), Gwenhwyvar-Guinivere as sovereign and dis-penser of material and spiritual goods, is the equivalent of the Grail guardian. Furthermore, in the later tale of the Cistercian Quest, when the quest requires procreation of an unsullied hero, Galahad (who will bring an end to these adventures), Lancelot of the Lake is made to sleep with the Fisher King's daughter, the bearer of the Grail. But, supposedly, in order to deceive Lancelot who is unswervingly faithful to Guinivere, the Fisher King's daughter is given Guinivere's appearance by magic. Basically, the Fisher King's daughter—bearer and guardian of the Grail—and Queen Gwenhwyvar-Guinivere are one and the same person from the mythological point of view.

An analogous scheme occurs at the beginning of Chrétien de Troyes *Erec*. Out of respect for custom, Arthur has carried out a "Hunt of the White Deer," a memory of an antique prehistoric ritual tied to a proto-Celtic religion characterized by cervid worship. Guinivere and Erec are off to the side where they meet a knight accompanied by a dwarf. These two individuals insult the queen's maid-in-waiting, and Guinivere feels that her honor has been impugned. Erec, at the end of his adventures thanks to which he had discovered the beautiful Enid, avenges the queen's honor by his victory over the abusive knight. The knight's name turns out to be Yder, son of Nut. The Welsh tale of *Gereint and Enid*, which corresponds to *Erec*, recounts the same incident and provides the Welsh—and Breton—name of the character: Edern, son of Nudd. Here we find ourselves in full Celtic myth. Yder is indeed well known. Under his ancient name of Edern (coming from the Latin *Aeternus*, "he who endures for a long time"), he became the Armorican-Breton Saint Edern, still represented in religious statuary as accompanied by a stag, and whose legend obviously retains traces of *cervidae* worship. His brother Gwynn (meaning White), son of Nudd, had a less pleasant fate. Being unable to get rid of him, Welsh Christians made him hell's door-man and a servant of Satan. As for the father, Nudd or Nut, he is the god Nodens seen in Gallo-Roman inscriptions throughout Great Britain, otherwise known as the Irish god Nuada of the Silver Hand, celebrated in ancient Gaelic epics. He appears quite often in the Arthurian cycle where he is one of Arthur's oldest companions. In addition, in the archaic French texts, the relations between Yder and Guinivere are some-what ambiguous.

In the Roman d'Yder, dating from the fourteenth century, King Arthur asks Guinivere one day: "If I disappeared you would be forced to take a man to defend you, but who would you choose from among my companions?" Guinivere thought on the matter and responded with Yder's name, prompting a sharp pang of jealousy in Arthur. An episode from the same romance shows Yder killing with his bare hands a bear that had entered the queen's chamber. Since the name Arthur contains *arto*, the word for bear, questions cannot fail to arise.

All of these are not idle considerations for they shed light on Guinivere's preponderant role in the Grail Quest. By all the evidence she is the starting point of the quest because she represents sovereignty. The gesture of the abusive knight alters that sovereignty: henceforth nothing can be as it was, hence the image of the Fisher King with his crippled legs who can no longer rule his kingdom effectively. Someone must avenge this affront *in the blood of the offender* and recover the cup. This episode that appears minor in *Peredur* (as in *Perceval* and *Parzival*) is, to the contrary, one of the major events of the story, for it irreparably sets into motion the process of the quest. This is the spirit in which English filmmaker John Boorman adapted the Arthurian legend for his film *Excalibur* (1981). He deliberately abandoned all the mystical aspects of the Grail and made the quest a reconquest of sovereignty. Indeed, the physically and morally wounded Arthur is no longer capable of ruling and his kingdom is going to hell. It is only when Perceval brings him the secret of the Grail ("the Land is the King," an eminently Celtic principle) that he regains his strength and sovereignty.

Thus Peredur is revealed as a witness to an event that will overturn the Arthurian universe. But since he is still quite unaware he doesn't even realize it. He only covets the weapons of the offending knight. He enters Arthur's hall on horseback and asks to be made a knight. At this moment a dwarf and his wife who have been mute for a year start to speak and greet the new arrival by his name, declaring him "the leader of warriors and the flower of knights" (Loth trans., vol. 2, 56), which is not to Kay's liking who slaps the dwarf and kicks his wife. Then, wishing to be rid of Peredur who has just spoken to him, Kay sends Peredur after the cup thief, telling him to obtain the thief's weapons. If he succeeds he can be dubbed a knight.

This episode is somewhat similar in Chrétien's tale, except there are no dwarfs: here they are replaced by a maiden who hasn't laughed for seven years. Kay, Arthur's foster brother and oldest companion, plays his customary role: he is the spoilsport always ready to pick a fight. In this regard he is the equivalent of a character from Irish myth, Bricriu of the poisonous tongue. In fact he represents the "bad conscience" of the collective. But in the later Arthurian texts, Kay, who was originally a formidable warrior endowed with magic powers, has become a kind of *miles gloriosus*, a braggart who is a wretched fighter.

Peredur doesn't dismount. He falls upon the thief of the cup, kills him, takes his weapons, and returns the cup to Owein (Yvain) requesting that he return it to Gwenhwyvar and that he also issue a challenge to

Kay on Peredur's behalf. He then leaves. In his errantry he defeats seventeen knights that he sends one after the other to King Arthur's court to be held prisoner and repeat his threats against Kay. Then one day,

> he reached a great, deserted forest; on the border of the wood there was a lake and on the other side of the lake a handsome fortress. On the edge of the lake he saw a white-haired man, with an accomplished air, clad in brocade and seated on a brocade pillow; his valets were in the midst of fishing. On seeing Peredur the white-haired man rose and made for the castle; he was lame. (Loth trans., vol. 2, 60)

It will be noted that Peredur hasn't yet encountered the woman Chrétien called Blanchefleur and Wolfram called Condwiramurs. The plot here is quite different. Furthermore, the fisherman is not Chrétien's Fisher King, but the hermit Gornemant de Goort. He is not paralyzed, he is merely lame. This physical blemish links him to a god from the Otherworld, the lame Indo-European god who sometimes appears as Haphaistos-Vulcan. And we will see that this fisherman—Peredur's uncle incidentally—is a kind of divine smith and dispenser of swords.

Peredur is warmly received by the fisherman who asks him if he is skilled with the sword. Peredur responds "I certainly believe if I were to be taught I would be quite skilled." The fisherman then puts him to a test: he has his two sons, one blond and the other brown-haired, "play at staffs" before him. Then he asks Peredur who, in his opinion, was the best. Peredur responds: "The blond could have drawn blood from the other if he had so desired." And his host then invites him to draw blood from the blond. Peredur takes his staff and capably "draws blood" from the blond-haired son, seeing which, the fisherman declares that he will teach him how to wield a sword and immediately dub him a knight. He then adds this piece of advice: "If you see something extrordinary, don't seek to question it until you have someone who knows enough to instruct you."

The episode bears the Welsh mark in the sense that the "sport of two-ended staffs *(ffon ddwybig)*" was one of the twenty-four national exercises of the Welsh. With Chrétien, Gornemant was satisfied with knighting Perceval and offering him discreet advice. Wolfram added an extra detail; the gentleman Gurnemanz had a daughter, Liase, whom he ardently wished to wed Parzival, who was, himself, not insensible to the young girl's charms. Wolfram must be using another model, at least it is a detail that Chrétien didn't keep and which the Welsh author transformed: the fisherman has, in fact, two sons, one blond and the other brunette, which is a sign of ambiguity. And knowing that at the end of the tale the bearer of the Grail is revealed to be the young male cousin of the hero, some questions are bound to arise. But nowhere else in *Peredur* is there an aspect that is as initiatory as this scene. And this is a bloody initiation; it is because Peredur succeeds in drawing blood from his blond cousin that he is accepted into the knighthood. Therefore the fisherman gives Peredur permission to go further, to undertake the quest. But he misleads him from another angle: he instructs him never to ask questions when he sees something extraordinary. It all plays out as if the fisherman wanted to ruin Peredur's visit to the castle of the Grail. Moreover, he adds: "It is not upon you that blame will fall but me, as I am your master" (Loth, trans., vol. 2, 62).

In sum the hero, as in shamanic initiations, is not entirely free in his actions. He is followed—both closely and from a distance—by the master shaman who is quite capable of lying to him (the hermit Trevrizent in Wolfram's story clearly lies to Parzival about the Grail), sending the neophyte on false trails, instigating his failures and reversals. But in the case of mortal danger the master will always be there to prevent any irreparable consequence to his pupil. This is often seen in folktales, particularly the famous Breton *Saga de Yann* in which the young hero achieves intiatory feats under the guidance—and surveillance—of a talking horse, who, in reality, is the young man's wizard father.*

But the lame fisherman is also a kind of smith. It is probable that this aspect was stressed more strongly in the archetype. However, traces of

---

* Markale, *La Tradition celtique en Bretagne armoricaine,* 148–68.

this original character remain in all the versions. With Chrétien, Wolfram, and the Welsh author, he teaches the hero to wield a sword and dubs him a knight. With the Welsh author he is lame and has two fairly mysterious sons. With Wolfram he has a daughter who wishes to unite with the hero. The reference to the daughter seems to come from an original Celtic outline found almost in its entirety in the Irish tale of *Finn's Childhood.** The hero named Demne (meaning deer) but surnamed Finn (meaning handsome, blond, thoroughbred), and the future King of the Irish Fiana, was pursued by the murderers of his father Cumal (the god Camulos of Gallo-Roman inscriptions). He was raised by women-warriors—like Cuchulainn, the hero of the Ulster cycle, and like Peredur who is later initiated by the witches of Caer Lloyw—who he has left to go rambling. He takes up residence with a master smith by the name of Lochan who has a very beautiful daughter named Cruithne. He weds the girl in an annual marriage, that is to say in legal temporary concubinage according to the Celtic custom, and asks Lochan to forge weapons for him. The smith makes him two spears and Finn can thus depart. But Lochan counsels him not to go "on the path where is found the trout named the Beo." Finn has nothing better to do than seek out this monstrous trout, kill it, and bring its head back to Lochan, "as a wedding gift for his daughter." Then he encounters an old woman who is mourning the death of her son at the hands of "a great and terrible warrior." Finn achieves revenge by killing the warrior, but as this is one of his father's murderers, it is a double vengeance. In addition it allows him to recover his father Cumal's treasure that the killer was carrying with him.

There are certain analogies between Peredur's quest and that of Finn. The theme of blood vengeance could not appear any more clearly. But this vengeance may only be achieved with a weapon that was given to the hero or forged during the course of an important stage of initiation.

* An English version of this can be found in *Revue celtique*, vol. 5, [Paris], 197 and *Eriu*, vol. 1, 180. An analysis and commentary of it is part of my *L'Épopée celtique d'Irlande*, 141–49.

When Finn received his two spears from the smith Lochan, he was in fact knighted, a rite that is obviously unknown in the Irish text, which is much more archaic than its Welsh counterpart. But the important thing is that from this moment forward, the hero is capable of accomplishing the still mysterious feat for which he seems predestined. However as a wise master, the fisherman-smith seeks to mislead him with his advice. Finn doesn't follow the smith's advice, which was what Lochan had undoubtedly forseen. But Peredur follows the fisherman's counsels to the letter. He is not yet capable of independence, he is not mature enough to respond with *no*. Hence the half defeat that follows.

For on the next morning—his period of initiation is of brief duration—he takes leave of his uncle and goes off. He arrives at another castle where the door stands open. He enters and is invited forward by an old man seated on cushions. After a meal the old man asks Peredur if he knows how to use a sword and he responds: "If one were to instruct me it seems that I would know." Then the old man shows him an iron crampon fixed in the room's floor "that the hand of a warrior could barely encompass." He gives him a sword and tells him to strike the crampon. Peredur obeys: the iron ring as well as his sword break in two. The old man tells him to "place the two pieces together and join them." Peredur puts them together and they become one as before. He strikes the ring a second time and it and the sword break anew. He again reunites the pieces. A third time he strikes the ring: the ring and the sword break again but this time it proves impossible to rejoin them. At this point the old man blesses him declaring: "You are the best swordsman in the entire kingdom. You have only two thirds of your strength, the third part is still wanting. When you attain your full power nobody will be able to contend with you" (Loth trans., vol. 2, 63–64).

This strange trial Peredur undergoes is very interesting; it is not only a question of destroying but rebuilding. Through his strength, Peredur is capable of breaking the ring and sword each time. But he requires the same amount of strength to rejoin the pieces. The third time he fails. Nevertheless, the old man recognizes him as the best swordsman in the kingdom. He will be capable of attempting the next test. It should be noted that the theme of the sword being joined together again is recognizable in the Cistercian version of the quest.

This is the point at which we come across the Grail procession again. The old man reveals to Peredur that he is his uncle, his mother's brother and thus the brother of the fisherman from the previous night. And then the mystery emerges:

> He had begun to converse with his uncle when he saw entering the hall and leaving for a chamber, two men carrying an enormous lance that had three streams of blood flowing from its socket onto the ground. All those in attendance began to cry and moan at this sight. Despite this the old man did not break off his conversation with Peredur; he gave no explanation for this event to Peredur and neither did Peredur ask for one. After a brief interval of silence two maidens entered bearing a large platter with a man's head on it bathed in blood. The company gave forth such cries that it was wearying to be in the same hall with them. In the end they quieted down. (Loth trans., vol. 2, 64–65)

That's all. There is no trencher as in Chrétien. The Grail is obviously not named: it is only a platter but what is important is what is seen on that platter: *a man's severed head bathed in its own blood.* In addition it is not merely a drop of blood that flows from the lance, but three streams of blood. Finally, the Grail, or platter rather, is carried by two young girls and those in attendance utter such cries of sorrow and lamentation that it cannot help but recall archaic funeral rituals of certain traditional societies.

It is a long way from this sober and precise tale to the rich Grail retinue described by Chrétien de Troyes. Wolfram von Eschenbach went even further in complicating the scene. It is probable that the Welsh tale is closest to the archetype, as we will see in the romance of *Jauffré.* Without embellishments and, especially, without any Christian connotation, this mysterious ceremony seems to surge, as if by enchantment, straight out of the deepest Celtic paganism.

For the severed head is a well-known motif from the oldest and most authentic Celtic tradition, as is testified to by archaeological finds as well as by the historical writings of the Greeks and Romans. Its importance to the understanding of Celtic religion and the Grail Quest make it necessary to devote some special commentary to it. As for the lance, which takes on its full value in the remaining portion of Peredur's tale, it is certainly not the lance of the centurion Longinius, as the Christianized versions of the legend have sought to claim. This lance is an equally well-known sacred object of Celtic mythology.

According to the Irish tale *The Battle of Mag Tured*, when the ancient gods, the Tuatha de Danann, arrived from "the Isles of the North of the World," they brought with them "science, magic, druidism, sorcery, and wisdom," but also various objects, one of which, Nuada's sword, we have spoken of in regard to Perceval's sword. The other objects are the Fal Stone, the Dagda's Cauldron (both of which we will have occasion to speak more of later), and the Spear of Assal: "From Gorias was brought the spear carried by Lugh; no battle could be won against it or he that held it in his hand" (Dottin, *L'Épopée irlandaise*, 17). In another tale, *The Fate of Tuirenn's Sons*, this spear is described with some curious details: it has a venemous and destructive power that can be reduced only by plunging the point of the spear into a cauldron filled with poison and "black fluid," blood, in other words. There it is, the Lance of the Grail, at least the spear of the original tale of the quest. It is also a magical spear. A poem (66) from the *Leabhar Gabala* (*Book of Conquests*, a verse summary of Irish mythology) instructs us that "dead is the person whose blood it spills. Its power is such that it cannot strike accidentally if only the word *ibar* (yew) is spoken. If *athibar* (also yew) is said it returns back to the hand of the one who cast it." The presence of this lance next to the severed head becomes perfectly justified if this scene is compared to a passage from the second part of the Welsh *Mabinogion*: During an expedition to Ireland, the hero Bran the Blessed is wounded in the leg by a poisoned lance (which is reminiscent of the Fisher King) and orders his companions to cut off his head and take it with them in order to obtain a kind of immortality feast.* In short, as we will learn further on, Peredur will be bound to avenge the death of the man whose head is on the platter, who was undoubtedly struck down by the bleeding lance. The lamentation forms part of a ritual that must be observed until this vengeance is achieved. It could not be said that the context of the original quest was particularly Christian.

But Peredur's adventures are far from over. Obviously he asked no questions. The next day he takes leave of his uncle and goes on his way. He meets his cousin, as in Chrétien's version, but here she is merely his foster sister. She treats him as if he were excommunicated, explaining to him that he bears the weight of his mother's death, but she says absolutely nothing about the enigmatic procession he has seen and does not reproach him for the questions he did not ask.

Peredur avenges his foster sister by sending her husband's murderer as a prisoner to King Arthur's court. He goes on his way with chance as his guide and traverses a land without animals that has been taken over by thickets. In the other versions this is the description of the countryside surrounding the Grail castle. But Peredur arrives at a castle where he is received by a young woman with whom he immediately falls in love: "She was wearing a tattered, old garment of brocade, that had once been good, and where her skin could be seen through it's holes it was whiter than a flower of the whitest crystal. Her hair and eyebrows were blacker than jet and in her cheeks were two small dimples that were redder than any other red thing" (Loth, II, 68). By all the evidence the author's description of this young woman was calculated to set the stage for the beautiful poetic imagery describing Peredur's ecstatic vision in the snow. In any case she is the same person as Chrétien's Blanchefleur except that the author of *Perceval* made her a blond.

Everything takes place almost exactly as it does in *Perceval*. The young girl comes in the middle of the night in search of Peredur ("I have come to offer myself to you") and explains her situation to him and requests

* Jeffrey Gantz, trans., *Mabinogion* (London: Penguin Books, 1976), 79–81.

his aid. Peredur promises everything, but in contrast to Perceval, does not have the girl enter his bed ("I will not leave you, though I don't wish to do anything such as you have offered until I learn from experience just what help I can give you"), and the latter returns to her room.

Peredur rids the young girl of her enemies by defeating them and sending them to King Arthur's court. He remains three weeks with his young girlfriend then takes his leave but promises to help her any time that she has need.

This episode is not quite identical to the corresponding episode in Chrétien's work, in which Perceval is genuinely and sincerely in love with Blanchefleur, nor to the one in Wolfram's book in which Parzival weds the beautiful Condwiramurs. In the Welsh tale, in fact, there is not even any question of sexual relations between the young girl and Peredur, who seems haunted rather by the image of an inaccessible woman.

Resuming his wanderings he meets the young woman from whom he had stolen the ring and effects a reconciliation between her and her lover. He next reaches a strange castle where he is welcomed by a countess surrounded by a large number of handmaidens. The countess invites him to dine but advises him not to spend the night because the castle is attacked every night by nine of the witches from Caer Lloyw (Gloucester). However, Peredur decides to remain. He is awakened by a terrible noise and fights one of the witches. He is on the point of killing her when she asks for mercy and tells him "I will give you a horse and arms. You will stay with me to learn horsemanship and how to handle your weapons." Peredur makes her promise that neither she nor the other witches would ever again attack the domain of the countess and, after getting the latter's permission, he leaves for Caer Lloyw where he stays three weeks in the witches' court.

This adventure takes place only in the tale of *Peredur*. It testifies to an incontestably Celtic source, but neither the romancer from Champagne nor the German poet retained it in their works since it calls into question the value that was attached to traditional chivalry, a tradition passed on by men after tests of masculine endurance. Now Peredur, who, let us not forget, had only two thirds of his strength, would acquire the last third from women. The French and German audiences could hardly have related to that. In contrast the Welsh author had no trouble including the adventure in his tale since it referred to an ancient Celtic custom whose memory had undoubtely endured in the Celtiphonic milieu, even in the form of legendary tradition.

For the witches of Caer Lloyw play the same role with Peredur as the women-warriors Scatach, Uatach, and Aïfe in the Irish story *The Education of Cuchulainn.** This is the decisive stage of his warrior's initiation. He learns not only the physical aspects of combat from these witches but also warrior magic, which seems so important in archaic societies. Peredur becomes virtually invincible because he receives communication of secrets, like the great epic heroes such as Cuchulainn, Finn, and even Siegfried and Achilles, who were initiated by women, as well. For Siegfried it was the Valkyrie while for Achilles it was his mother, Thetys. Henceforth Peredur can acquit himself of his mission successfully.

He still doesn't know which road to travel, but it doesn't seem that Peredur ever had a very clear idea of his mission. His first stay at the Grail Castle did not leave behind an imperishable memory. After choosing a horse and weapons, he leaves the court of the witches and goes on his way haphazardly. He visits a hermit, but the text says almost nothing of this event, which Chrétien took much more into account and which was developed even further by Wolfram von Eschenbach. This is the meeting with Trevrizent, another uncle of Parzival, who, in giving the hero additional information about the Grail, deceives and misleads him even further.

This brings us to Peredur in the snow-covered field adjacent to the place where King Arthur has established his camp. Having seen the raven drinking the blood upon the snow, he thinks of she whom he loves and falls into ecstasy. It is not very clear just which woman Peredur is thinking of: "The woman he loves best" is not very informative, and

---

* Markale, *L'Épopée celtique d'Irlande*, 88–95. See also the previous chapter on Chrétien de Troyes for material concerning Perceval's encounter with the young girl of the ring.

Peredur's quest is liberally scattered with women who love him and with whom he falls in love. In any event she is a brunette. It is possible that it is simply the ideal image of Woman that he pursues and has not yet encountered, similar to the famous sylph that imbues all of Chateaubriand's work.

Arthur sends his companions to invite Peredur to their campsite. He knocks them end-over-end, one after another, Kay in particular, in order to be left alone to his reverie, until Gwalchmai-Gawain succeeds in coaxing him to accept Arthur's invitation. Peredur is given a celebration by King Arthur. But on the next day he meets a young woman, Ygharat Llaw Eurawc (Ygharat, or Angharad Golden Hand). He tells her: "I could love you more than any other woman if you wished" (Loth trans., vol. 2, 83).

A priori, Peredur's attitude seems quite fickle. Each time he meets a young woman he falls in love, thereby forgetting the previous ones to whom he has said almost the same thing. The first justification is psychological. Peredur is not in search of the Grail, since he has forgotten the Lance and the mysterious platter, but of the Ideal Woman, the projected image of the brown-haired goddess found again in the romance *Jauffré*, in which case the quest for the Grail, that has been given such mystical and Christian interpretations, could only be a "quest for the woman," after all. This is the search for a feminine deity, concealed by patriarchal societies, then Christianity itself, but whose resurgence is visible in the spread of the cult of the Virgin Mary in the twelfth century. A second justification is mythological. The young woman with the ring, the young woman analogous to Blanchefleur, the countess, and Ygharat Llaw Eurawc are, in reality, only manifestations of a single woman who appears later in the text under the title of the Emperess, a sovereign and initiator, Peredur's veritable "mistress," who is the equivalent of the strange and ambiguous Cundrie of Wolfram von Eschenbach. A third justification, finally, is of a social and ethical order. Celtic societies, heir to druidic conceptions, didn't possess the same notion of amorous fidelity as the strongly Christianized societies in which sex is burdened with an extreme sense of guilt.

The problem turns around an essential question: Is it conceivable that absolute love, as vaunted in Celtic texts and the medieval texts they inspired, carries with it an obligation of exclusivity, or, to the contrary, can it touch a number of individuals?

Study of Celtic texts allows one to respond that fidelity in love didn't exist. The tale of *The Education of Cuchulainn* and that of *The Courtship of Emer* show us Cuchulainn engaged to the woman he loves best, Emer, yet still leaving for initiation with the women-warriors of Scotland with whom he will have temporary but real sexual relations. The same Cuchulainn, in the tale *The Illness of Cuchulainn*,* falls in love with the fairy Fand, rejoins her in the Otherworld, and remains with her over a certain period of time. But, called upon to choose between Fand and his wife Emer, he decides in favor of Emer despite his desire for Fand, saying: "By my word, it is you that pleases me and will continue to please me for as long as you shall live." Queen Medbh, heroine of numerous epics, has countless lovers on whom she bestows "the friendship of her thighs," but only for winning the service of warriors of whom she has need, without lessening her preference for her husband Ailill. The same is true for Guinivere: though she is madly in love with Lancelot of the Lake, she is no less "faithful" to her husband Arthur. The attitude of Iseult toward her husband King Mark is not very clear despite the "absolute" love that binds her to Tristan. And Gawain, the model easygoing knight, is ready to perform the most difficult feats in order to prove to the latest maiden he meets that he loves her more than the others. Peredur belongs to this same category: he promises Ygharat no more than to love her more than the others. He reacts exactly as a traditional Celt would. But the same cannot be said for Perceval and Parzival who are already prisoners of the Christian ethic.

The Celtic notion of fidelity is especially one of relativity. Overall it is a fidelity to a chosen individual, truly the freely chosen individual that is loved with an absolute love in a privileged relationship that suffers no other relationship of the same type. This principle thus stated, the passing or temporary relationships that could affect either one of the two

---

* Dottin, *L'Épopée irlandaise*, 117–41. Markale, *L'Épopée celtique d'Irlande*, 122–28.

making up this ideal couple are only of very secondary importance. They are necessarily of a different nature, political, social, economic, quite simply sexual, or even, in what seems to be the case for the famous Courtly Love of the twelfth and thirteenth centuries, purely familial. Indeed, the love that binds the lady to her lover is not comparable to that which binds the Lady to her huband, the Lord, clarifying, moreover, the relationship between the lover and the husband, and between the vassal and the suzerain, giving a good conscience to the lover and safeguarding the husband's self-esteem. It is for having reneged on this principle that King Arthur, in the last part of *Lancelot* known as *The Death of King Arthur*, bears the primary responsibility for the dislocation, then annihilation, of the fellowship of the Round Table, when he no longer accepts Guinivere and Lancelot's liaison, expelling the latter and depriving himself of Lancelot's essential participation in their common work. This was the shape taken by the analysis made by the nineteenth-century Utopian philosopher Charles-Louis Fourier in *L'Attraction passionée*. There he sheds light on what he names with no underlying motive the "pleasure party," concluding that these kinds of infidelities have little importance.

> Everyone comes to agreement by means of some trivial verbiage and one enters into an accord of *sixte*, in which each person knows the respective infidelities and dual utilizations of love. There a new bond is established, that tacitly accepts this phanerogamous accord, that balance of amorous contraband in which each finds his proper wage.

It would, moreover, be high time to research the origin of Courtly Love, or more correctly stated "Fine Love," in the mores and customs of Western Celtic societies rather than in vague Arabic contributions, these contributions being purely literary whereas the Celtic contributions are from the domain of the sociology of daily life.

Whatever the case may be, the episode of Ygharat Llaw Eurawc is only found in *Peredur*. From this point forward the Welsh tale becomes very different from the tales of Chrétien de Troyes and Wolfram von Eschenbach.

After his declaration of love to Ygharat, Peredur hears the the young girl's answer: "I give you my word that I don't love you nor will I ever want you." This couldn't be clearer. However, Peredur is not discouraged. He swears this oath: "I give my vow that I will not speak to any Christian until you confess that you love me better than all other men" (Loth trans., vol. 2, 83). And Peredur abandons the court to throw himself into a new period of errantry.

In a forest he passes by black houses of rude construction and sees a lion chained at the edge of a deep pit filled with the bones of men and beasts. He breaks the lion's chain and topples the beast into the pit, and then reaches a valley where a castle is located. In a meadow he sees a large gray-haired man and two young lads—one blond and the other brown-haired—who are busy throwing knives with hilts of walrus ivory. Peredur realizes that the lion was the gatekeeper of the gray-haired man. This man amiably invites Peredur to stay but his host's daughter reveals to him that on the next day he would be forced to fight the giants that dwell in the black houses and are her father's vassals.

Of course the old, gray-haired man is a double of the Fisher King. He has two sons—one blond, the other brown-haired—and supposedly a daughter (we will see later that the character is fundamentally bisexual), and Peredur, wandering aimlessly, finds himself plunged into a new set of tests. It certainly seems that these tests are not designed to prove his valor but to lead him astray: since he neither knows where he is going, nor knows his goal, it is paradoxical but indispensable that he be able to discover himself and reanimate within the images that lurk in his unconscious mind. Peredur therefore fights the giants and kills a third of their number. He even kills the two sons of his host, who then begs him for mercy. Peredur grants it to him on condition that he go to King Arthur's court and have himself baptized. Since the inhabitants of this castle are not Christians, the hero was able to speak with them without breaking his oath. He resumes his journey. He hears a serpent speaking who is sleeping on top of a ring. He doesn't hesitate: he kills the serpent and takes the ring.

The author is hardly explicit on the episode of the snake and the ring, but it is a prefiguration of something that will occur a little later. The symbol of the serpent and the ring is obviously sexual: by killing the serpent, Peredur eliminates the male element, the father in other words, to the benefit of the female element represented by the ring, a maternal token if there ever was one. Let us not forget that Peredur, as well as Perceval and Parzival, must perform an as yet undefined deed within his mother's family. In this instance he makes a choice between belonging to the family of his father (patriarchal society) and belonging to the family of his mother (gynecocracy). And his choice reflects the Celtic components of the story.

Following this episode he meets Arthur's knights who do not recognize him and to whom he cannot reply because of the conditions of his oath to his absolute love. He again wounds Kay and is called the "Mute Valet." It is then that Angharad Llaw Eurawc appears. She doesn't recognize him either, but she says: "It is a great pity that you cannot speak; if you could I would love you of all men best, and, by my word, though you cannot, I will love you best all the same" (Loth trans., vol. 2, 89). Peredur, filled with joy, answers that he loves her. Her declaration has freed him of his oath. Everyone recognizes Peredur who remains at King Arthur's court in the company of Gwalchmai, Owein, and the other knights. But the author says nothing further concerning Angharad Golden Hand.

One day while hunting with Arthur he becomes lost; he stumbles upon a dwelling where some valets are playing chess and he seats himself there next to three maidens. One of them warns him that the master of the house kills anyone who ventures into his home. Of course the master, a black, one-eyed man, forces Peredur to fight the next morning, after granting him a night of grace on his daughter's intervention. But Peredur is victorious and asks the black man how he became one-eyed.

By all the evidence Peredur is in the "underworld." His host is a cyclops. This is also the image of the great Indo-European god that is master of time and space, the great Germanic Odin-Wotan, the historicized Horatius Coclus of Roman annals. The black man has therefore subjected Peredur to a test through which the latter has acquired the right to know where he should go.

Indeed the black man explains to him that he became one-eyed by battling with the Black Serpent of the Barrow: "There is a hillock called the Cruc Galarus (the Sorrowful Mound), and on that barrow is a cairn, and in that cairn a serpent, and in that serpent's tail a stone. The stone has the virtue of giving whomever shall hold it in one hand as much gold as that person could wish in the other" (Loth trans., vol. 2, 91–92). And he tells Peredur the road he must take to reach a mysterious Countess of the Feats. Then Peredur kills the black man in cold blood, upon which one of the maidens tells him that he is now owner of all the treasures of the castle and can choose the woman there that pleases him.

The detail concerning the stone in the tail is quite intriguing. This marvelous stone bears a strong resemblance to the Philosopher's Stone of the alchemists, all the more so as the dragon's tail was a symbol readily used in the treatises of traditional alchemy. Additionally, the theme of the underground treasure guarded by a serpent or a dragon (then by a devil) is very widespread in oral folklore.

But to reach the cairn in which the serpent dwells, Peredur must pass by the Court of the King of Suffering. It will be noted that this name offers a certain resemblance with the Méhaigné King (that means the king who is maimed or suffering from his wound) who is a double of the Fisher King in the Christianized versions of the Grail Quest. Furthermore the events that take place in this castle are not without a connection to the Grail.

> On entering he saw only women. They rose upon his arrival and gave him a warm welcome. He began conversing with them when he saw a horse coming that carried a corpse on its saddle. One of the women got up, took the corpse from the saddle, bathed it in a tub of warm water that was near the door, and then she rubbed it with a precious ointment. The man came back to life and warmly greeted Peredur. Two more corpses arrived in their saddles and the woman revived them as she had the first. (Loth trans., vol. 2, 94)

This is not the lone example of a tub in Celtic tradition. It can be seen again in Ireland, where, following the Battle of Mag Tured, it was capable of restoring "the heat to warriors who had been killed in such a way that they were fully alive on the next day" (G. Dottin, *L'Épopée irlandaise*, 23). It was called the Fountain of Health. In the second branch of the Welsh *Mabinogion* there is a cauldron with this property: "If a man is slain today, you have only to place him inside and tomorrow he will be as alive as before, except he will no longer have the power of speech" (Loth trans., vol. 1, 129). This coupled with another cauldron in the Welsh tradition that procures inspiration and abundance can't fail to bring to mind the healing properties of the Grail that, according to Chrétien and the authors of the continuations, feeds and maintains the life of the wounded king. This theme of the Celtic cauldron is so important that it deserves an entire chapter of its own.

On this occasion Peredur does not remain stupidly mute before such a strange spectacle. He demands an explanation. He thus learns that the young men were killed every day by an *addanc* that lived in a grotto. The next day when the young men set off to fight the *addanc* again, Peredur asks to accompany them. They refuse, saying that if he was killed no one would be able to revive him. Peredur is satisfied to follow them at a distance.

This *addanc* belongs to the fabulous bestiary of Welsh tradition. Sometimes called an *addanc* and sometimes an *afang*, it denotes a monster, a kind of serpent or dragon, whereas in reality the word means "beaver." A widespread tradition, but one of uncertain origin, made a monster of this lake- or pond-dwelling animal that was constantly gnawing away the dikes and causing floods. It can be seen that the famous Loch Ness monster is not merely an invention of a journalist in need of a story, but, in reality, refers to ancient beliefs.

It is at this juncture that Peredur has a major encounter in his quest. Again it is a woman. Indeed he sees, "seated on a mound, the most beautiful woman that he has ever seen." This woman tells him:

I know the aim of your journey, you are going to fight the addanc.

He will kill you, not with valor but with cunning. There is a stone pillar at the threshold of his cave. He sees everyone who comes without being seen by them and, from the shelter of this pillar, he kills them all with a poisoned sting. If you give me your word to love me more than all other women in the world, I will give you a stone that will allow you to see it when you enter but it will not see you. (Loth trans., vol. 2, 94–95)

Peredur gives her his word in saying that he has loved her from the moment he first saw her. And to the question "Where will I find you?" the woman replies: "You will look for me in the direction of India." And she disappears after placing the stone in Peredur's hand.

The setting for this episode is a megalithic mound. Resurfacing here are ancestral beliefs concerning the mounds, the famous *sidh* of Ireland, abode of the ancient gods, heroes, fairies, and supernatural beings, a privileged place where treasures are concealed. But entering these mounds is always a perilous undertaking, hence the intervention of the mysterious woman. Who is she? We will find out later, but it is possible to conjecture that she is one of the appearances of the feminine deity who has been assisting the young hero from the beginning of his long quest. Peredur has no difficulty loving her and promising to love her more than any other. She is not described in this scene but it can easily be imagined that she was a brunette. And she is truly a fairy or a sorceress, since she gives Peredur the stone of invisibility, comparable to the ring of Cyges and the ring that the fairy handmaiden Luned gave to Yvain in *The Knight of the Lion* by Chrétien de Troyes.

In any case we have here a traditional theme that is widespread throughout the entire world. When Theseus fought the Minotaur, he did so in an underground labyrinth, but was only able to do so victoriously thanks to a woman, Ariadne, who gave him the famous thread. When Jason took possession of the marvelous Golden Fleece, he only did so thanks to a woman, the sorceress Medea, who put the sacred object's dragon guardian to sleep (Dottin, *Les Argonautiques d'Orphée*, 38–40). And in the Hittite tale, "The Dragon Taken by Cunning," the goddess

Inara asks the mortal Hupasyia to kill the dragon of the depths, but Hupasyia only accepts the mission on condition of becoming the goddess's lover, in order to obtain a little of the divine power necessary to accomplish the feat (T. H. Gausser, *Les plus anciens contes de l'humanité*, 122–23). On each occasion, the aid of a woman—the keeper of divine or magical powers—is indispensable for the success of the undertaking. As in the numerous folktales in which the hero is given a magical object—or spell—by a woman he has met, Peredur has now gained enough maturity to further his quest.

But this quest unfurls in strange countries. Peredur arrives in a valley where a river is flowing.

> On one bank there was a flock of white sheep and on the other a flock of black ones. Each time a white sheep bleated a black sheep would cross the river and turn white and each time a black sheep bleated a white one would cross the river and become black. On the bank of the river stood a tall tree: from roots to crown one half was covered with flames, the other half bore green leaves. (Loth trans., vol. 2, 95)

One cannot help but compare this scene to the one described in the Irish tale of *The Voyage of Maelduin*, whose manuscript goes back to around A.D. 1100.

> They spotted a new island with a spiked palisade dividing it in half. There were many sheep, a black flock on one side of the palisade and a white flock on the other. And they saw a fat man who separated the sheep. When he threw a white sheep over the palisade it immediately became black. In the same way, when he threw a black sheep over the palisade it immediately became white. (J. Markale, *L'Épopée celtique d'Irlande*, 198)

As for the detail of the tree that is green on one side and in flames on the other, it brings to mind the well-known medieval legend of the Dry

Tree as well as the long dissertation contained in the tale of the Cistercian Quest on the Tree of Life, brought by Eve from the Earthly Paradise.*

It is not difficult to realize that Peredur now found himself on the frontier of two worlds, that of the living and that of the dead. But according to the Celtic concept there is constant exchange between the two worlds. This conforms perfectly with the druidic beliefs such as were known by Greek and Roman authors: "Death is only a point in the middle of a long existence" (Lucian, *The Pharsalia*); "souls do not perish, but after death they pass from one body to another" (Caesar); "souls are immortal and live again for a certain number of years in another body" (Diodorus Siculus); "souls are immortal and there is another life in the land of the dead" (Pomponius Mela). And it is known that on the eve of Samhain—the great Celtic feast of November 1—there was total intercommunication between the two worlds, "for the *sidh* of Ireland were always open on Samhain and nothing in the *sidh* was hidden" (*Finn's Childhood*).

What needs to be considered is that these exchanges between the two worlds *go in both directions:* humans on entering the Otherworld truly become beings of the Otherworld, and the folk of the Otherworld become humans. This is what most stands out from the symbol of the black and white sheep. And all metamorphoses are possible here.

But three routes are available for Peredur to take. He asks directions from a young hunter and makes his way to the addanc's cave. Thanks to his stone of invisibility, he has no trouble slaying the monster and he returns to take his leave of the three sons of the King of Suffering, declining their invitation to stay and wed one of their sisters.

At this point he is joined by a knight in red armor, Edlym Gleddyfcoch (Edlym of the Red Sword) who declares himself Peredur's vassal and asks to accompany him. They are welcomed to the court of the Countess of Feats. There it was custom that anyone who

---

* Albert Béguin, trans., *La Quête du Saint Graal,* (Fribourg and Paris: 1945), 176–92.

could overthrow her three hundred men would have the right of sitting at her table. Peredur succeeds at the test and, as the Countess is in love with the red knight, "that very night, Edlym and the Countess slept together."

The next day Peredur and Edlym set out for the Sorrowful Mound. Around the mound they find three hundred men who are awaiting the death of the serpent so that they may fight among themselves over the ownership of the stone in the serpent's tail. Peredur fights against these three hundred men, besting them all, then goes, as he puts it, "to pay a visit to the serpent," kills it, and takes possession of the famous stone that provides gold. By its virtue he distributes riches to the three hundred men on condition they become his vassals. Then he gives the stone to Edlym and recommends he rejoin the Countess and remain at her court. Then he is off once more, the eternal vagrant, in search of who knows what.

It will be noted that Peredur didn't keep the stone for himself. He still wasn't quite sure of just what he was destined for. He continued his search, but the riches procured by the stone do not seem to have been a sufficient goal for him.

Peredur arrives at a spot where he sees a countless number of windmills and watermills, and he meets the head miller who gives him lodging. He learns that the Empress of Constantinople has assembled all the knights of the world there on the plain in order for them to compete with one another in tournaments, so that she may choose as her husband the most valiant among them. Peredur goes to the tourney and sees the Empress, "the most beautiful maiden in all the world," and of course falls madly in love with her. He displays his love by triumphing over all the other knights and sending them to the Empress. Finally she receives him. During this reception three men come who will each present her with a cup of wine to give to the individual that will fight them in succession. The Empress gives the cups to Peredur who slays his three adversaries. Then the Empress says to him: "Kind Peredur, do you remember the promise you made me when I gave you the stone that allowed you to slay the addanc?" (Loth trans., vol. 2, 103). And then Peredur rules with her for fourteen years.

The three cups of wine are obviously a reminder of the one that unleashed Peredur's quest: Queen Gwenhwyvar's cup. Peredur is now at the peak of his powers and strength. He has become the invincible warrior and the Empress takes him as her husband. A curious character this Empress: she herself admits having given the stone of invisibility to Peredur, and yet Peredur did not recognize her, which didn't prevent the hero from falling in love with her. It is basically understood that all the women encountered by Peredur up to now are different aspects of the same woman, this Empress, a strikingly clear image of sovereignty and supernatural power.

Peredur's adventures could end here. This "marriage" between Peredur and the Empress is a kind of conclusion. By this reckoning the quest would essentially be a Quest for the Woman. And it could be said that the Welsh author preferred to abandon the model he shared with Chrétien de Troyes to branch off into a totally different tradition, since, starting with Peredur's meeting with Angharad, the plot is completely different. Or else a case could be made in which Chrétien deemed it inadvisable to retain the adventures from this part of his model as these adventures were not at all Arthurian and were too strongly marked by their Welsh context. However, despite their character that is apparently foreign to the quest of the Grail, all the adventures from this part of the story serve to reinforce the initiatory aspect of Peredur's itinerary. In any event, the element of blood vengeance seems absent; undoubtedly Peredur must achieve his quest for the Woman before attaining his ultimate goal.

Yet, it is also from this moment forward that the Welsh tale finds itself abruptly back in the Arthurian context, becoming for a time parallel to Chrétien de Troyes's *Perceval.*

We are now at the court of King Arthur, in Caer Llion ar Wysg (the old capital of Britannia seconda in South Wales). Peredur, rigged out in his customary cognomen Paladyr Hir (long lance), finds himself in the company of Gwalchmai, Owein, and Howel, son of Emhyr of Brittany. All at once a young, ugly, black-haired damsel arrives, mounted on a yellow mule. She is the equivalent of Chrétien's hideous Maiden on the Mule and Wolfram's Cundrie.

> Her appearance was rough and coarse; her face and hands were blacker than pitch, she had high cheeks and a sagging face with a small, wide-nostriled nose, one eye sparkling gray and green, the other black as jade and sunk deeply in her head; she had long teeth as yellow as broom flowers. In front, her chest stuck up higher than her chin and her backbone was shaped like a cross. (Loth trans., vol. 2, 103–04)

This horrible maiden has a friendly greeting for everyone but Peredur against whom she lashes out in anger. Basically she tells him:

> You went to the court of the lame king and saw the young man with the red lance, with a drop of blood that transformed into a torrent flowing down to the young man's fist; other marvels you saw there yet asked neither their cause nor meaning! If you had done so the king would have obtained health for himself and his dominions. (Loth trans., vol. 2, 104–05)

Now it can be understood what Peredur's true test was during his visit to the mysterious Castle of the Severed Head. He would have been able to establish contact between this odd world, a kind of undifferentiated Otherworld, that was sterile in any case, and the world of the living from which he had come. He would have been able to revive a dying land and restore fecundity to a kingdom that had become sterile due to its king's impotence. The lame king is the symbol of royalty. As it turned out, Peredur wasn't capable of prompting communication and instigating a dialogue between the inhabitants of this mysterious region and the living whom he represents. This theme can be discovered in numerous legends and folktales. The hero arrives by chance in a sunken or vanished city. He is always solicited by the inhabitants to buy something or answer questions. Unfortunately, the ignorant hero either has no money with which to buy anything, or doesn't know the answers to the questions asked, or does not himself ask any questions. Then the city disappears and the hero finds himself alone once more, despairing over his missed opportunity and haunted by the desire to again find the path that led to this strange location.

But the Ugly Maiden adds that, for anyone who wishes to cover himself with glory, there is an exceptional opportunity: in her dwelling, Proud Castle, reside five hundred and seventy knights prepared for combat, and on a mountain not far from there is a young maiden held prisoner in a castle. "He who delivers her will have the greatest fame throughout the world." Immediately Gwalchmei declares that he wishes to free the young maiden while Peredur says: "I will not sleep in peace until I know the history and meaning of the lance that the dark lady spoke of" (Loth trans., vol. 2, 106).

Thus are drawn up the two quests: that of Gawain is directed toward the young woman held prisoner, but that of Peredur, who has already completed the quest of the Woman, has as its objective the answer to the questions that he had not asked. What is remarkable here is that he is more preoccupied with the Bleeding Lance than by the Severed Head on the Platter. Which just goes to show that the "Grail" can be quite different depending on the individual seeking it.

Gawain's quest in the Welsh tale is very simplified and even very condensed in comparison to the redundant nature of Chrétien de Troyes's text. There is no mention of Arthur's mother and his actual freeing of the young maiden isn't witnessed by the reader. The tale leaves Gwalchmei-Gawain at the moment he sets up his engagement with the knight who accused him of killing his father and henceforth the tale is entirely devoted to Peredur. But there again, there are no more parallels between the Welsh text and Chrétien's text, there is only the fact that several episodes are included in the *Continuations*.

Peredur wanders across all of Britain seeking news of the dark young woman. But no one can give him any information. At the end of one day's wandering he asks his blessing from a priest who refuses because he is carrying arms on Good Friday. He however excuses

Peredur, who had forgotten what day it was, and gives him lodging.

This is the lone passage of this last part of the book that is common to the Welsh author, Chrétien, and Wolfram. Peredur asks his host questions about the Castle of Wonders, that is about the castle where he himself had witnessed the mysterious procession. The priest advises him to go to the other side of the mountain where there is a royal court in the valley; he would surely learn something there.

Peredur reaches the court. He is warmly invited in and shows himself so attentive to the king's daughter, who appears to welcome his advances, that the king has him seized and thrown in prison. But the daughter comes to rejoin him during the night. It is again she who supplies him with arms and armor so that he may participate in the combats taking place between the king's men and those of a very powerful count who has risen in revolt. He promises her that he will return to the prison that evening. Peredur kills the count's men then the count himself. True to his word he returns to the prison where the king's daughter takes pains to see he gets his "warrior's rest" that night. Finally the king's daughter tells her father that the victor was none other than his prisoner. The king frees him and offers him his daughter as well as half his kingdom.

But Peredur refuses, satisfied with asking for information concerning the Castle of Wonders. The king's daughter exclaims: "The ambition of this man is higher than we dreamed." After telling him that he is the man "she loves best," she gives him directions: "Cross yonder mountain, and you will see a lake with a castle at its center, and that is called the Castle of Wonders. We know the name but we know nothing of the wonders" (Loth trans., vol. 2, 114).

The theme of the castle at the center of a lake, and often even under the lake, is very widespread in Celtic mythology and folktales. It is a magic domain, a kind of Otherworld that can only be entered by the one who knows the entrance. In the Irish tale *The Expedition of Loegaire*, the heroes dive into a lake and see a fortress and countryside comparable to those of the Earth's surface (Dottin, *L'Épopée irlandaise*, 33). In another Irish tale, *The Pursuit of Gilla the Hard*, the heroes of the adventure visit the "Land Beneath the Sea" (Markale, *L'Épopée celtique d'Irlande*, 152).

In the Welsh *Story of Taliesin*, there is a certain Tegid the Bald: "His dwelling was at the center of Lake Tegid and his wife's name was Keridwen" (Markale, *L'Épopée celtique en Bretagne*, 95). In the *Reductorium Morale* of Pierre Bercheur—Latinized fourteenth-century author—the knight Galuagnus (Gawain) can be seen diving into a lake and discovering a strange fortress. As for Lancelot of the Lake, according to the tale from the *Vulgate* (as also in the original version of *Lanzelet*; see J. Markale, *La Tradition celtique en Bretagne armoricaine*, 119), he was raised in a marvelous country by a "water fairy," the "Lady of the Lake," otherwise known as Vivian. And let's not forget that Arthur's sword Kaledfwlc'h (Excalibur) comes from the lands beneath the water.

Peredur reaches the castle to which he was given directions. In fact it is not the true Castle of Wonders, but a first stage on the way to reaching it. The gates are open. He enters the hall and sees a game of chess: "The two sides were playing against each other by themselves; the side he helped lost and the other side's pieces shouted, absolutely as if they were real men. This angered him so he gathered the pieces in his lap and threw the board into the lake" (Loth trans., vol. 2, 114–15). At this a young "black" girl appears who scolds him for his deed and informs him that he has lost the Empress's chessboard that she values more than all else.

This strange chessboard, a prefiguration of the modern electronic chessboard, merits a brief pause for further study. First of all, the episode appears again with much more detail in the *Continuation de Perceval* by the pseudo-Wauchier, as well as in *The Quest of the Holy Grail:* here a beautiful water fairy emerges before Perceval but the story is the same. Welsh tradition classes among the thirteen marvels of the Isle of Britain "Gwendoleu's chess game: one has only to stand the pieces on the board and they will play by themselves." This is certainly the same magic chessboard and it brings to mind this scene from the Irish tale of *The Voyage of Art, Son of Conn*, in which the young Art plays chess against his father's concubine, the fairy Becuna Cneisgel who is aided by the invisible folk of the *sidh* who move the pawns and are responsible for her victory (Markale, *L'Épopée celtique d'Irlande*, 187).

It is true that the Celts played the game of chess, or at least a game similar to chess (*fidchell* in Ireland) passionately. But the game acquired a symbolic value as well. In fact the prominent role of the queen—the true power of the game—says a lot about the equivalence that exists between the class and gender structures of the original Celtic society, as do the rules of the game itself: the king, the one indispensable piece, can do almost nothing.

This is in conformance with the type of role played by the Celtic king, who can only speak after his druid has spoken, who must be present at a battle for the battle to be won but cannot take part, and who is the pivot of a society for which the queen is the sole embodiment of sovereignty.

This chessboard episode is obviously a test imposed upon Peredur by the Empress herself. The young "black" girl is yet another face of this Empress who is perpetually present in Peredur's quest. And it is a test for accession to royalty for which a Dutch tale from the fourteenth century, *Gawain and the Magic Chessboard*, furnishes proof.

Arthur and his companions are assembled in a hall. A flying chessboard comes in the window and leaves again by the same. Arthur promises his kingdom to whomever brings back that chessboard. Only Gawain attempts the adventure and pursues the chessboard, which disappears into the side of a mountain. Gawain enters the mountain and is forced to fight dragons. He then finds himself in a magnificent castle whose master, King Marvel, promises him the chessboard on condition that he bring back the marvelous sword of King Amaoren. Gawain succeeds in obtaining the sword and receives the magic chessboard that he then gives to Arthur, but we are not told if Arthur left his kingdom to his nephew (*Revue des Traditions populaires*, vol. 31 [Paris], 164–70). The basic theme of this story can be found in numerous European folktales.

This adventure of Peredur can be explained as follows: placed in the presence of the chessboard he is unable to resist and plays the game. His invisible adversary is obviously the Empress, and she wins because she is the sovereign. But Peredur as a man cannot accept such a situation or such an inferior condition, hence his angry gesture: he would rather destroy than take second place. However, this dislocation of the kingdom is a catastrophe for everyone. Hence the warning from the young black girl that obliges Peredur to recover the chessboard. But by doing so he will prove to the Empress, and himself, that he is capable of assuming royal duties. All this is a reduced outline of the Grail Quest, during the course of which Peredur must provide proof that he is capable of restoring life and prosperity to a kingdom that has become sterile as a consequence of the death or impotence of a king, whether he proves it through the accomplishment of an act of blood vengeance or through the cure of the wounded king.

After having reproached him for his act, the young "black" girl tells him what he must do to recover the chessboard: he must go to Caer Ysbidinongyl. "A black man there ravages a great part of the Empress's domains. By killing him you will get the board. But if you go there, you will not return alive."

Usurpation and oppression are the themes here. Since the kingdom has been broken apart—by the fault of Peredur—legitimate power has been weakened thus allowing the oppressors to ply their personal ends. It is thus up to Peredur to restore order. But this is a perilous enterprise in which his life is at risk, for when oppression is allowed to develop there is always a risk that it will get out of hand. In short, this part of Peredur's tale, which only appears fairylike, actually provides a political lesson.

Peredur finds the black man, fights him, and grants him his life if he will restore the chessboard to its rightful place. But the young black girl reappears and curses him for leaving the black man alive. Indeed, those who would disturb an organized society should be eliminated in no uncertain fashion. Peredur retraces his steps and kills the black man. After which he asks the young girl where he may find the Empress. She answers that he will only see the Empress when he kills a stag that has been destroying men and beasts in the forest. But it cannot be slain unless it is flushed out by the Empress's spaniel.

The stag is a diabolical animal here. Ancient deity of the prehistoric deer hunters that became Cernunnos for the Gauls, always portrayed with horns, recuperated by Irish legend under the guise of Finn (whose real name is Demne, the deer), his wife Sadv (half-woman and half-doe), his son Oisin (the fawn) and grandson Oscar (the deer lover), the animal retained a certain ambiguous nature in the Christian Middle Ages. Though it appeared in an episode from *The Quest of the Holy Grail*, as completely white with a gold collar and surrounded by four lions to portray Christ and the four Apostles, most often it served as an image of the horned and hair-covered medieval devil. This is the sense of the image we see here with an even more profane meaning: it is the very symbol of the oppression and injustice suffered by the kingdom that Peredur, if he is truly the righter of wrongs he claims to be, must eliminate completely.

Peredur makes his way to the forest guided by the spaniel. He ambushes the stag, kills it, cutting off its head, and starts to carry it away, when suddenly a knight looms up who steals the head and spaniel and disappears. Peredur immediately goes in pursuit of the knight, who reproaches him for killing the best thing in his realm, the stag, and will only consent to giving Peredur back the dog on the condition that he go to a bush on the mountain. There he will find a flat stone (a dolmen in other words), where he will have to fight against whatever lives beneath it. A black man emerges from beneath the stone mounted on a skeletal horse. They fight, but the black man jumps on his horse and, taking Peredur's horse with him, vanishes completely, leaving Peredur totally disconcerted.

These adventures are developed much more fully in *The Quest of the Holy Grail*. There an old woman makes off with the head and the dog. To recover the dog Perceval fights a man who has emerged from a tomb, but another knight steals the head and dog from the old woman. He cannot find either his adversary or the thief again. Greatly vexed he goes in search of the old woman who tells him that he is not in the know about anything and then disappears with the laugh of a young girl.* But

* Albert Pauphilet, trans., *La Quête du Saint Graal* (Paris: Lib. Anc. Hon. Champ., 1967), 45–51.

it is especially in the *Second Continuation of Perceval* (by the so-called pseudo-Wauchier II) that the story of the chess game and the events that followed acquire a great importance. It forms the very framework of the tale and at the end it is the Lady of the Chessboard herself—equivalent to the Empress—who gives the stag head back to Perceval and welcomes him quite amorously to her castle. By all the evidence, the *Second Continuation*, despite its excessive Christianization, follows the same model used by Peredur's author quite closely.

Throughout this story it is the Empress who guides the plot. She drags Peredur through phantasmagorical and incomprehensible adventures where he is at risk of losing his way, but she does this for the purpose of guiding him through the magical landscapes that mask the Castle of the Grail. The same is true in Wolfram von Eschenbach's book, since it is Cundrie the Sorceress who reveals the path to Munsalvæsche to Parzival. It is only after following many twists and turns, many detours and reversals, and many oversights that Peredur is ready to accomplish the mission for which he was destined.

He walks the length of a valley where he spots a castle next to a river. He enters the castle and is surprised to find his own horse in the stable, next to Gwalchmei's horse. He makes his way to the great hall and finds Gwalchmei there in the company of an old lame man, in other words the Fisher King. We are not told what adventures brought Gwalchmei-Gawain to the Castle of Wonders, and especially how he was able to get there before Peredur. But there is one thing, however, that Gwalchmei cannot accomplish that is reserved for Peredur alone: vengeance.

This vengeance forms the central theme for the story of *Peredur*. The hero, after being seated next to the crippled king, sees a young blond man who comes to kneel before him. These are the strange words he speaks:

> It was I who came to Arthur's court in the guise of the young black girl, and who appeared again when you threw away the chessboard, when you killed the black man from Ysbidinongyl, when you killed the stag, and when you battled the man from the flat stone. It was

again I who carried the bloody head on the platter, and the lance with the stream of blood that ran down its shaft from its point to my fist. The head was that of your first cousin. He was killed by the witches of Caer Lloyw; it was they who lamed your uncle as well. I too am your cousin. It has been prophesied that you would take revenge. (Loth trans., vol. 2, 118–19)

It is thus clear that it is not the blood of Christ, nor the lance of Longinius, nor any form of esoteric mysticism with which we are dealing in the Welsh version of the story. To the contrary it is the sociological element that is preeminent, as Celtic legislation—in Wales as in Ireland—allowed for personal revenge and made a sacred act of it. This certainly seems to be the case here. In addition, there is a close-knit relationship between the ideas of vengeance and healing: in old Irish, healing and payment are expressed by the same word (*iaccaim* that can mean "I pay" or "I cure"), and the same is true in Welsh *(iachau).* Let us not forget that in the *Parzival* of Wolfram von Eschenbach, the hero, when leaving his mother, is overheard saying that he must get his revenge on Le Hellin. We will also see in the romance of *Perlesvaus* that the hero achieves his revenge in conditions strangely reminiscent of an ancient Gallic ritual sacrifice.

But it is in the *Third Continuation* by Manessier that everything is clearly expressed. There Perceval kills a certain Partinal of the Red Tower, cuts off his head, and gives it to the Fisher King. The wounded, lame king upon seeing the head, *rises up on his feet completely cured* and thanks Perceval for having avenged him on his enemy. This conformity with the text of *Peredur* permits one to feel that the framework of the original quest was exclusively one of a blood vengeance that enabled the healing of a wounded king and the restoration of life and prosperity that had become sterile because of its sovereign's impotence.

But what's to be said of the Woman and her role in the quest? Her role is essential since it is only by virtue of the clues she supplies, the tests she advances, and the magical-sexual initiation she administers that the regeneration, which is the quest's objective, occurs. Wagner was not in error with the development of the magnificent and strange character of Cundrie in his Parzival that is otherwise rendered so dubious by the philosophical implications it contains. From the beginning Peredur finds his path marked out by women: his mother, first of all, who gives him her famous pieces of advice, the young girl with the ring, the young girl who is Blanchefleur's equivalent, Angharad of the Golden Hand, the young girl carrying the severed head, the first countess surrounded by ladies-in-waiting, the witches of Caer Lloyw, the young woman who treats him as an outcast and who is the equivalent of his cousin, the woman who gives him the stone of invisibility, the Countess of Feats, the Empress, the hideous Maiden on the Mule, the count's daughter, and the young black girl who is associated with the chess game and the knight who makes off with the stag's head and the dog. It's a long list. But aren't we dealing with the same woman under different guises here?

One has the right, though, to ask questions as to the very nature of this woman since the young blond-haired male cousin of Peredur comes before him and claims that he was himself several of these women, to wit the hideous Maiden on the Mule, the young girl with the chess game and the knight, and especially the one who carried the severed head, otherwise known as the Grail bearer. The least that can be said is that this character is characterized by a remarkable sexual ambiguity. In short, when this character is feminine she has the appearance of a young brown-haired girl, corresponding to the ideal Peredur is seeking. But when this character is masculine he appears under the guise of a young blond-haired man. In all likelihood the two aspects are complimentary and represent night and day, shadow and light. But as the Celtic philosophical system is a monism, which considers beings and objects to be simultaneously one and multiple, and which refuses any dichotomy either on an intellectual level or on the level of daily behavior, it can be asserted that this apparent phantasmagoria on the part of the Welsh author has its source in Celtic tradition. And it is because these Celtic elements were incomprehensible to a non-Celtic, Christian, twelfth-century audience that they were not retained by Chrétien de Troyes and his successors.

This does not explain the reasons for this bisexuality. Certainly

Peredur-Perceval's personality is in itself ambiguous, sometimes very feminine, but in no case homosexual. The most probable explanation is that it was a case of ritual androgyny. Indeed, Peredur's woman of countless faces—let's call her the Empress—is a supernatural being, or a sorceress, at the very least, since she can change shape. She belongs to the Otherworld and manifests according to the criteria that have the best chance of attracting Peredur's attention. She is the reflection of the Deity, the Goddess of the ancient Celts periodically seen reappearing as various legendary characters such as Guinivere, Iseult, Morgana, or Vivian. And, since she needs to be embodied, this deity is also the priestess. The Empress has the characteristics of a priestess, but since in the end she turns out to be a man, she has to be a shamaness, or better yet a shaman, since it is known that shamans dress in women's clothing wishing to show by their dress that they share two natures, (masculine and feminine), and that they are a reflection of the original Androgyne, symbol of the individual in Paradise Lost, before the great separation (the etymological meaning of sex) occurred. The goal of shamanism being the restoration—whether in a symbolic manner, speech, dream, or ecstatic trance—of the primordial state of existence, it could be said that the Empress plays the role of shaman who leads the hero to the ardently desired regeneration. In short, what Peredur learns at the Castle of Wonders is that the Individual is One, above all, and that bisexuality, far from being a blemish, monstrosity, or sickness, is the realization of this forgotten reality.

Meanwhile, Peredur has yet to achieve the final deed that will complete his quest. Peredur and Gwalchmei appeal to Arthur and his companions to attack the witches of Caer Lloyw. They engage in battle. Peredur, who possesses the same powers as the witches since they initiated him, prevents them from slaying Arthur's men. Furthermore, it seems that his role was limited to this alone. Just as the witches could do nothing to him, he could do nothing to them, save prevent them from killing those who were achieving his revenge. Thus Peredur's presence proves indispensable to this combat and it is his presence that permits his cousin and uncle to be avenged. Everything has been completed: the witches, representing the disturbing world of magic and the warrior formulas of an earlier time, are annihilated. But it mustn't be overlooked that Peredur himself is keeper of the secrets of the sorceresses, the one and only keeper. Here, perhaps, is where the idea of a Grail Royalty resides.

The Romance of *Perlesvaus*

Like numerous works from this time, the composition date of the tale entitled *Perlesvaus* has been disputed. After having established that a contemporary but parallel text, *The Quest of the Holy Grail*, appeared around 1230, its composition has been placed between 1190 and 1195 in Britain under the direct influence of Glastonbury Abbey, and consequently in the sociopolitical influence of the Plantagenets who wished to make this abbey the major center of Arthurian tradition, truly the Isle of Avalon itself. Let us not forget that, because of searches ordered by King Henry II, the tombs of King Arthur and Queen Guinivere—whom the Plantagenet always claimed as their ancestors—were discovered at Glastonbury. Medievalists have, for the most part, judged *Perlesvaus* as a very secondary work of the Arthurian Cycle, a badly constructed imitation burdened with unbelievable elements that is not worthy of inclusion in the Grail tradition. It's as if only Chrétien de Troyes, Wolfram von Eschenbach, and the author of *The Quest of the Grail*, the so-called Walter Map, have any right to speak about the Grail. The Grail, however, is one of those mythological objects that belongs to the entire human race, and for each person the essential thing is determining what meaning one wishes to give it. In contrast to *Peredur* and *Jauffré*, the Grail appears and is named in *Perlesvaus*. And the name of the hero changes, as well. This troubles the usual exegetes of the Grail as its meaning, Perdles-vaux (lose the valley), brings us back to the original quest: a story of ritual blood vengeance. Perceval, or more exactly Peredur, was a reassuring name because it was more or less impenetrable. By his very name Perlesvaus destroys the soothing vision of the imbecile hero who accedes by chance to the mysteries of divine ecstasy, because Perlesvaus knows what he wants. His mother told him that his mission was to avenge his father and to kill an enemy guilty of ransacking his domains. His name is the observation of his situation: he has lost the "valleys" that his heritage consists of; it is up to him to reconquer them in order to regain his full and complete identity.

At bottom this reconquest is the principal subject of *Perlesvaus* and it can be achieved only through blood. Rarely has a "courtly" work been more bloody and violent. This is the reason that the composition of the tale can be dated before the Cistercian recuperations. The Cistercians were contemplative mystics and *The Quest of the Grail* by the so-called Walter Map bears the indelible mark of their pacifist mysticism, already accentuated by Robert de Boron, the true transformer of the original quest. Only fragments of his work remain available to us such as the famous *Didot-Perceval* and the *Huth-Merlin*. This Cistercian spirit is totally absent from *Perlesvaus*. On the other hand, the concept of the crusade, dear to the Cluny Orders, is clearly present here. Glastonbury, as is known, came out of the Cluny Orders. Consequently, Perlesvaus can only be situated between Chrétien de Troyes and the Cistercian transformation of Robert de Boron, that is to say, between 1190 and 1195. Here Clunysian violence met Plantagenet determination to build upon blood and strength, an empire inherited from the legendary King Arthur with all of its social, political, cultural, and religious components. The beginning of Perlesvaus's adventures is borrowed from Chrétien de Troyes, but beginning with the moment that the hero first enters the Castle of the Grail the framework, without being fundamentally different, becomes charged by elements unknown to Chrétien de Troyes and the Welsh author of *Peredur*.

Indeed, through the fault of Perlesvaus who has not asked the expected questions, the Fisher King falls into a state of decline and the entire country is struck by a curse: for if the king is incapable of ruling, the kingdom can no longer function normally, a perfectly Celtic notion that establishes identification of the land with the king. But this curse is much more dreadful because even the court of King Arthur becomes stricken as a result. The king loses his ability to bestow gifts, in particular, which causes the abandonment of his court.

It is known that the gift was an extremely important social element for the Celts and that the king is the keeper of this gift-giving ability. It is even the essential role of the Celtic type of king; he must give, otherwise he is good for nothing. It thus seems that the curse brought about by Perlesvaus's missed opportunity was of a profane as well as a religious nature. All of Arthurian society is affected by it, bringing us back to the initial episode in Perceval's, Jauffré's, and Peredur's quests in which the sovereignty embodied by Guinivere is flouted.

It is precisely Guinivere who attempts to do something. She advises King Arthur to make a pilgrimage to the Saint Augustine Chapel in Wales (this chapel belonged to Glastonbury Abbey). An invisible force prevents the king from entering the chapel but outside he attends a Mass and even has a celestial vision. On his return he triumphs over a knight carrying a flaming lance and sees that he has regained his power to bestow gifts. He decides to hold court in Penzance, in Cornwall. There, three messengers come from the Fisher King who describe their master's misfortunes, the state of his kingdom, and the mission an audacious knight would have to accomplish in order to restore things to their original condition. These messengers leave behind a shield that had belonged to Joseph of Arimathea for Perlesvaus.

Thus the character of Joseph of Arimathea makes his appearance in Arthurian legend and in context with the Grail. No one, before the author of *Perlesvaus*, had yet established a relationship between the Grail and this somewhat enigmatic figure from the Gospels. Certainly it is known that this Joseph of Arimathea, a member of the Sanhedrin (Luke 28:50), "who was a disciple of Jesus, but in secret out of fear of the Jews," had asked Pilate permission "to take the body of Jesus down from the Cross" (John 19:38). With Pilate's permission, Joseph had taken Jesus down from the Cross and entombed him in a grave that he had intended for himself, hollowed in the rock (Matthew 27:60). But in the texts of the Vulgate there is no mention of anything else, and certainly no mention of some kind of container in which he would have collected the blood of Christ. Medically speaking this would have been impossible, but that hasn't prevented certain authors of apocryphal books—or those judged as such—from stating this. This is how the pseudo–Gospel of Nicodemus, the *Gesta Pilati*, and the *Vindicta Salvatoris* echo the traditions concerning this "collection" of Jesus' blood by Joseph of Arimathea. And Joseph, arrested by the authorities for suspicion of sympathy for the agitator Jesus, would have been, while in prison, the keeper of this precious vessel, brought to him by an angel and allowing him to survive. It is from all of this that Robert de Boron pulled the great lines of the classic legend of the Holy Grail, and quite successfully, as is known. It is important, however, to know that the name Arimathea means "the tombs," which casts a shadow of doubt on the authenticity of this character.

However, after the intervention of the three messengers of the Grail, who are a three-faced version of Chrétien de Troyes's famous Maiden on the Mule, presented here in a typically Celtic trinitarian form (there are countless depictions of mother-goddess triads in Gallo-Roman statuary), the knights of King Arthur decide to throw themselves into the Quest in order to reestablish the normal condition of the kingdom.

Gawain learns that he must first win the sword used to behead John the Baptist. He obtains this relic after battling and killing a giant who had kidnapped the son of the pagan king Gurgalan, the sword's official guardian. Gawain returns with the relic just as Gurgalan decides to convert, along with his people, to Christianity. But since Gawain was unsuccessful in his attempt to prevent the giant from killing the young son of the king, the latter is given a bizarre funeral: his body is cut into strips and boiled in a cauldron, following which all those attending the funeral drink this odd broth.

It cannot be claimed that this tale, despite its obvious Christian influence, conforms to Christian dogma and custom. The reference to Saint John the Baptist provides an interesting link between *Perlesvaus* and the Grail procession in *Peredur* during which a severed head on a platter is displayed to the hero. This is clearly associated with the severed head ritual and the pagan element incontestably predominates, even though the traditions concerning Salome and John the Baptist are truly Christian.

In addition, the fact that Gawain must obtain a marvelous sword before discovering the Grail Castle fits into the category of Celtic quests for objects from the Otherworld, objects it is necessary to obtain before committing oneself to the final stage leading to the successful conclusion of the undertaking, the typical model for this, of course, being the Welsh tale of *Culhwch and Olwen*. Finally, even though *Perlesvaus's* author drew a parallel between the Last Supper of Good Friday and the consummation of the king's young son, it is difficult not to see in it the memory of an ancient pagan anthropological ritual for which Irish stories provide specific examples.

Armed with this sword, which is some kind of "golden bough" for gaining access to the Otherworld, Gawain crosses the perilous bridges leading to the Grail Castle where he is received by the Fisher King. The light from the Grail is as bright as day. There are twenty-two knights in the hall, who are all over one hundred years of age but appear hardly forty. A magnificent meal is served. Two maidens appear—one holding the Lance, the other holding the Grail—followed by two angels bearing candelabras. Gawain is so awed by this sight that he falls into a swoon of ecstasy and forgets to ask the questions that the Fisher King himself had requested he ask. Everyone looks at him sorrowfully. The procession again passes before him but this time there are three angels and a childlike shape within the Grail. Gawain cannot pull his eyes away from three drops of blood that the Lance left on the table. Then the Grail is hoisted into the air and Gawain sees the image of the crucifixion, with Christ's side pierced by the lance. Gawain remains there alone. Before him is a chessboard whose pieces move by themselves. Gawain moves the pieces but is beaten twice. In anger he breaks the game, which then disappears. He falls asleep. The next day he finds the doors shut and tries in vain to enter the chapel where Mass is being said. A voice then announces to him that the king of Mortal Castle, faithless and renegade brother of the Fisher King, is going to attack the Grail Castle. Gawain discovers his horse ready and saddled, and departs into a raging tempest.

Gawain's quest was a failure. He hadn't asked the necessary questions, either. Yet he had brought the sword. He had been instructed beforehand what he must do. We are told that the cause of his failure was his awed and ecstatic reaction to the unreal sight he witnessed. But wouldn't it rather have been because Gawain knew too much intellectually? There seems to be an antimony between knowledge and actual life experience here. Gawain, though tightly linked to the Quest, is not the chosen one. He is only the forerunner. It will also be noted that the Grail appears quite Christianized here but it doesn't contain the blood of Christ. This would be rather the blood that dripped from the Lance. Finally we are informed that the Grail Castle is going to be the target of the faithless and traitorous brother of the Fisher King. Because of Perlesvaus's failure the Fisher King had slipped into a state of decline and decay. Because of Gawain's failure the entire kingdom will be subjected to misfortune. No one has the right to fail at a quest; personal failure unleashes a collective decline.

Gawain's adventure is significant: the Grail may well be the object of his quest but it is not its essential element because everything comes into play within the quest itself. One can gain access to the Grail in a relatively easy fashion but it is all for naught if the end result of the quest is negative. Gawain's experience illustrates this and Lancelot of the Lake will find himself constantly confronted by the same kinds of problems.

Indeed, Lancelot of the Lake in turn sets off on his own search for the Grail. He enters a devastated city, the City of Weapons or Souls [Armes and Ames, respectively, in French—translator's note] whose air is filled with the wails of invisible beings. A knight holding a large two-handed ax asks Lancelot to cut off his head with that weapon and return in one year to undergo the same fate. Lancelot accepts the challenge but on leaving he sees that the head and body have disappeared.

This City of Souls is obviously the Grail Castle disguised under another fleeting appearance, one perhaps meant to force Lancelot to undergo a trial of courage. The invisible voices wailing in this devastated city brings to mind the cries heard by Perceval during his first visit to the Castle of Wonders, and the manifestations of collective grief witnessed by Jauffré at Monbrun. As for the "decapitation game" that Lancelot is forced to undergo, it is of undeniably Celtic origin. In a famous Irish tale, *Bricriu's Feast,* the hero Cuchulainn is confronted with the same test (Markale, *L'Épopée celtique d'Irlande,* 112), and the same is true for Gawain in two Arthurian texts, one French, *Gauvain et le Vert Cavaliere,* the other English, *The Green Knight.* This theme refers to the very curious Severed Heads ritual.

Continuing his quest Lancelot reaches the Grail Castle such as it appeared to Gawain, where he is also received by the Fisher King but neither the Grail nor the Lance are paraded before him. He goes to receive confession from the Hermit King, Perlesvaus's uncle; in fact, it is the sin of adultery that he committed with Queen Guinivere that held the Grail away from him. The hermit then tells him that if he had truly desired to see the Grail with the same force he desired the queen, he would have seen it. Lancelot responds ambiguously, however; if I am interpreting his words correctly they seem to say that for Lancelot the goal of the quest is Guinivere who represents all that is most beautiful and noble in this world. In sum, if Gawain undertook his quest to prove his prowess, Lancelot undertook an amorous quest in which the sacred, mysterious object represented by the Grail was replaced by the erotic object depicted by Guinivere.

However, Perlesvaus, the one responsible for the Fisher King's infirmity, has also undertaken this quest that will confront him with countless perils. He meets the Hermit King his uncle, who is here named Pellés. Perlesvaus is constantly changing his armor to intrigue and confuse everyone whose path he crosses in the course of his wanderings. It certainly seems that this changing of armor could be a rationalized transposition of a much older myth; indeed, Cuchulainn in Irish epic myth is continually changing his appearance and even his shape. When seized by warrior fury he enters into a transformative trance before hurling himself against his enemies. While in the midst of one of his famous contortions he earned the surname "The Contortionist from Emain" (Dottin, 105; Markale, *L'Épopée celtique d'Irlande,* 100–101).

Perlesvaus secretly enters Arthur's court at Penzance during the night and takes away the shield left for him by the Fisher King's messengers and the sword brought back by Gawain. He gives aid to Lancelot, who is on the verge of being overcome by an attack of some formidable brigands, and meets his sister who informs him both of the Fisher King's death and the momentary disappearance of the Grail. This is the point at which Perlesvaus has the opportunity to successfully complete the initial quest that prompted his departure from his mother's home; she had in fact asked him to avenge himself on the enemies that had wrested possession of their domains after killing Perlesvaus's father. Perlesvaus will gain his revenge in a very surprising fashion. He decapitates twelve of his enemies and collects their blood in a cauldron. He then hangs the chief of his enemies upside down in the blood-filled cauldron so that he suffocates and drowns. It cannot be said that this bloody ritual is in conformance with the Gospels and the Christian spirit of the twelfth century that Perlesvaus's author claims to exalt. No Christian exegesis can justify a ritual murder of this type, the archaic and pagan nature of which is beyond doubt. Equally curious is the author's relentless need to demonstrate that Lancelot's failure is the result of his sensuality, unequivocally condemning both adultery and sexual relations while magnifying Perlesvaus's bloodthirsty attitude, which is not exempt from a certain sadistic quality. Is this to say that the Cluny monks, who had a visible influence on the author, preached violence? Absolutely, the Cluny Order was a promoter of the Crusades, a bloodbath in itself, but it must be said as well that the Church's attitude has always been quite clear. Corresponding to its rejection of sexuality and the fanatical association of guilt with that activity, is an acceptance, if not to say a benediction, of war and its consequences. This hypocritical attitude of the Church, this alliance "of the Sword and the aspersorium" that has been denounced so often and that is so contrary to the evangelical spirit, has manifested throughout the course of history but perhaps most strongly at the end of the twelfth century. At bottom, chivalry, naively presented to us as an "ideal" and even as a "mysticism," was only the recuperation by the Church and those in power of people's most bloodthirsty instincts, using them to achieve ends that were much more temporal than spiritual in nature. It is quite easy to understand why the pacifist movements of the twentieth century issued their famous slogan "make love not war." The animating spirit of Perlesvaus's tale is clearly the opposite: "make war not love."

Despite this, Perlesvaus's vengeance, over which the author smugly extends himself* seems to emerge straight out of the archetype that is common to *Perceval, Peredur,* and *Jauffré.* If Chrétien and the author of *Jauffré* were more discreet on this matter, the author of *Peredur* has allowed a great many details to stand, proving the reality of a blood vengeance ritual: the systematic massacre of the Caer Lloyw witches that is the final episode—and the conclusion of the quest—provides a striking example. And the torture inflicted on his enemy by Perlesvaus is nothing other than a ritual sacrifice of Celtic paganism.

Indeed the scholias of the Latin text *The Pharsalia* by Lucian, a work that incidentally provides much useful information on Gallic religion, makes mention of a sacrifice in honor of the god Esus that involves hanging a man by his feet over a cauldron until he suffocates. And one of the plates carved on the famous Gundestrup Cauldron seems to illustrate this scenario with the idea of resurrection added. In another instance an Irish story, *The Adventures of Nera,* extremely interesting for its archaic nature, recounts this kind of torture and seemingly links it to the great festival of Samhain on November 1. It is difficult to believe that the author of Perlesvaus invented this detail; he borrowed it from Celtic archetype or, at the very least, from the model in French that preceded *Perceval* and *Peredur* to which the latter text had remained quite true. After all it is not impermissible to think that the hero of the original Quest, whatever his name was, was a Celtic priest, a druid, and that the quest itself was the literary story of a bloody ritual in honor of the god Esus, whose name, or surname rather, corresponds to the Latin legend *Optimus,* meaning the best or the very good.

Perlesvaus returns to Arthur's court where he receives a triumphant welcome. One would think his adventures were ended. But everything starts over. A mysterious Dragon Knight has dared to challenge Arthur and all his knights. Here we find once more the starting point for the

---

* William A. Nitze, ed., *Perlesvaus,* (Paris: Champion, 1927), verse 5330 ff.

quests of Perceval, Peredur, and Jauffré. A lady whose lover has been killed by the Dragon Knight promises the "Golden Circle" to he who will avenge her. Perlesvaus accepts the challenge.

Meanwhile, Lancelot enters a contest that puts his head at stake in the City of Souls. Like Cuchulainn in the Irish tale, he only undergoes a simulated decapitation. And Perlesvaus forces the gates of Castle Turning whose enchantments he breaks. Thanks to his courage, but thanks also to Joseph of Arimathea's shield, he vanquishes the Dragon Knight but is burned by the flames of the dragon. His wounds heal when he puts on them the ashes of the knight—and lover of the lady—who had himself been completely burned away by the dragon. The lady then gives Perlesvaus the mysterious Golden Circle, another aspect of the "golden bough" that allows entry into the Otherworld.

Thus Perlesvaus has succeeded at another quest. After so many trials he has reached a higher rank in his initiation. He is actually the avenger, but by seeking revenge for others and not himself, he transcends himself. This is also the reason that he can be healed by the ashes of the knight who fell victim to the dragon. But here again the theme of healing through vengeance is clearly visible: it is because he has killed an enemy that he is purified, therefore capable of undertaking the last stage of his quest.

Perlesvaus finds himself before another magic fortress, a Tower of Copper. It dissolves before him as he draws near. We are, of course, dealing here with Perlesvaus's victory over his own illusions, the unhealthy images that prevent him from seeing past his customary horizon. Once again he sees his uncle, the Hermit King, who gives him a mule with a starred forehead. This mule leads him to the Castle of the Grail. But to free the castle it is necessary for him to fight against the renegade brother of the Fisher King, the master of Castle Mortal. As he advances toward his enemy that latter individual kills himself with his own sword and falls into the water that surrounds the castle. Again Perlesvaus has defeated his illusions. In reality the master of Castle Mortal was only the projection of the unhealthy terrors that encumber the minds of heroes.

Then the Grail and the Lance reappear in the castle along with the priests and knights who were there before the kingdom's decline. The Fisher King is interred within a chapel that is miraculously illuminated every night. At Carduel where he is holding court, King Arthur is fore-warned of Perlesvaus's success by the appearance of two suns in the sky. And one curiously learns that the unknown murderer of Arthur's son is none other than the seneschal Kay, but he has time to escape.

It is probable that the author of *Perlesvaus* is blending various tra-ditions here. The hero, in the terms of his quest, has rid the Grail Castle of the obscure veil that encompassed it, a veil symbolized here by the oppression of the master of Castle Mortal. In some manner he has become king of the Grail and acquits himself of his duty by having his predecessor buried. But why churlishly introduce this story about a murder of King Arthur's son, a murder committed by Kay? Only the Welsh tradition makes reference to a son of King Arthur (outside of Mordred, Arthur's incestuous son who will cause both the king's death and the disappearance of the Arthurian world). In fact, according to Welsh tradition Arthur had three sons but it is not specified whether they were of Guinivere. The Latin text of the *Historia Britonnum* makes note of a certain Gwadr, slain by the magic boar Twrch Trwyth, and a certain Amr, killed by Arthur himself in a combat in which he hadn't recognized his opponent (a very common theme in mythological tra-ditions). The same *Historia Britonnum* gives the name of a third son, Llacheu, a proud warrior that one of the *Triads of the Isle of Britain* classed among the three men of that island who had invented new things (Triad 27). But it's the text of *Perlesvaus* that is the most explicit on this subject. Llacheu had the annoying habit of falling asleep after he killed an enemy. Now one day, after he had killed the giant Llongrin, he fell asleep on the corpse. Kay passing that way felt his jealousy aroused at Llacheu who was his equal in valor and toward Arthur who sometimes treated him with too much derision. Kay then slew Arthur's son in cold blood and cut off the giant's head, which he brought back to Arthur as proof of his prowess. Therefore Arthur believed that Kay had killed the giant thus avenging Llacheu. But once the Grail was rediscovered by Perlesvaus the time of such impostures was at an end.

This may be one of the meanings of the original Quest, as well.

Arthur decides to make a pilgrimage to the Castle of the Grail. Then Queen Guinivere dies suddenly to the great despair of Lancelot. Arthur, however, undertakes his pilgrimage. While en route the king and his companions sleep in a deserted dwelling in which they find the severed heads of two hundred men. The house is haunted by diabolical phantoms who Arthur, Gawain, and Lancelot succeed in routing. This anecdote, parallel to the final episode of *Peredur* in which Arthur's men massacred the witches of Caer Lloyw, is a sort of propitiatory ritual; it points out the necessity of purifying the kingdom of all its hidden diabolical elements before one may gain access to the great transparency of the Grail.

Perlesvaus welcomes Arthur to the Castle of the Grail. During a mass the Grail appears in five different forms that cannot be spoken of for one mustn't speak of "the secret things of the sacraments." This detail is reminiscent of the prayer that the Hermit King teaches to Perceval in Chrétien de Troyes's text. But the author tells us, anyway, that the fifth form is that of a chalice. It is the first time, according to this author, that a chalice has been seen in Great Britain (Nitze, ed., verses 7181–7237). And it is also the first time in the Grail texts that the sacred object is portrayed as a chalice; one sees whence came the Grail containing the blood of Christ.

However, Arthur's knights spin intrigues against Lancelot of the Lake who, inconsolable, goes to collect his thoughts at Guinivere's tomb at Avalon, openly identified as Glastonbury. Perlesvaus leaves the Castle of the Grail to perform yet another mission; his mother's enemies are still alive and he continues to fight them. He pursues a certain Aristor in particular, who was the murderer of his uncle Pellés, the Hermit King, and who also sought to marry the hero's sister by force. Here again we can clearly see that blood vengeance is an omnipresent element of the Quest. Perlesvaus has become the king of the Grail, a saintly and divine figure, and keeper of the most precious object in the world, nevertheless he continues the vendetta that seems to be at the origin of every story of the Quest.

Once his revenge has been achieved Perlesvaus climbs aboard a boat that mysteriously brings him to the Castle of the Four Horns or the Four Corners. There white monks show him a glass coffin in which the remains of an armed knight rest, who is none other than Joseph of Arimathea. Perlesvaus learns that he can only leave this castle after solemnly swearing to return upon seeing a boat whose sail is marked by a red cross. Perlesvaus so swears and he is admitted to a table of gold and ivory. A golden chain hangs down from the sky that is laden with precious stones, and in the center of that chain is a gold crown.

Here is an episode that is not lacking in interest. As noted before, the history of the discovery of Arthur's son's murderer denotes a Welsh influence. For the moment we are fully in Welsh tradition, and what's more, this can provide us a valuable indication concerning the origin of the archetype of the original Quest and that quest's objective, in other words the "receptacle" of multiple names and shapes.

Indeed, if one carefully registers the details provided by *Perlesvaus's* author (who claimed to have translated them from a Latin manuscript preserved on the Isle of Avalon, that is to say, Glastonbury), one will note: a water journey of somewhat marvelous aspect but well within the Celtic tradition of the pilotless boat, a castle of four corners, a glass coffin, precious stones, and a chain that hangs down from the sky. That said, one can cite these verses of poem 30 from the famous Welsh manuscript called *The Book of Taliesin*, which dates from the thirteenth century but contains much earlier texts that have been, rightly or wrongly, attributed to the sixth-century bard Taliesin:

> *Complete was the imprisonment of Gwair in Caer Sidhi by*
> *the vengenace of Pwyll and Pryderi.*
> *None before had been able to enter the city.*
> *A heavy blue chain preserved the courageous young man*
> *who sadly sings among the remains of the Abyss . . .*
> *Was I not promised glory if my song be heard?*
> *To Caer Pedryfan, the four-walled citadel, this was the first*
> *word expressed by the cauldron.*

He is sweetly warmed by the breath of nine maidens.
Is this not the cauldron of the Master of the Abyss?
At its summit are circles of pearls.
It doesn't provide food to a coward, that is not its role.
A sparkling, manslaying sword was extended to him and in
*   the hand of Llyminawc was left.*
Before the gate of hell, a lamp is burning.
When we went with Arthur on his noble undertakings, but
*   for seven, none returned from Caer Fedwyd . . .*
Was I not promised glory if my song be heard?
At Caer Pedryfan, on the isle of the Powerful Gate, where
*   the twilight and the fountain of night commingle,*
the drink was a sparkling wine borne before the procession.
Three times full the ship Prytwen took us upon the sea, but
*   for seven, none returned from Caer Rigor, the citadel of*
*   the royal assemblies.*
I will not sing the praises of the masters of literature for far
*   from Caer Wydr, they have not witnessed the feats of*
*   Arthur.*

The elements that appear both in the text of Perlesvaus and the Welsh poem are extremely specific. It is a journey over water that brings the hero or heroes to the mysterious citadel. Caer Pedryfan means literally the "City of the Four Sides," and later on it takes the name of Caer Wydr, which means "City of Glass." A comparison can be made between this city and the glass coffin in which Joseph of Arimathea has been laid to rest, but in any event the City of Glass is the name given in numerous tales to a fortress of the Otherworld, such as the Kingdom of Gorre or Voire, Meleagant's domain in Chrétien de Troyes's *Knight of the Cart.* We thus find ourselves within an illusionary castle both in *Perlesvaus* and in the Welsh poem where mention is made of the Abyss (Annwfn in Welsh), which can also be interpreted as the word "hell" or "inferno" in the non-Christian sense of the term. The heavy blue chain in the Welsh poem corresponds to the chain hanging from the sky in *Perlesvaus.* The precious stones in the French story have their counterparts in the circles of pearls in the Welsh tale. There are too many corresponding details for these to be mere coincidences.

This is not all. Other observations emerge. Gwair's imprisonment in the quadrangular city can be compared to the fact that Perlesvaus cannot leave the Castle of the Four Horns or Corners, unless he promises to return. The name of Gwair has often been cited as an equivalent to Gwalchmei-Gawain, but it is possible to see him as the hero of the original Quest. As for Pwyll, it is the Welsh form of the name Pellés, which is disturbing enough in itself. And what then is this homicidal sword if not the same as the sword of Perceval or Peredur, or even, in later versions of the Quest, the Sword of the Strange Belt, with which will be struck the dolorous blow that wounds the Fisher King and causes the sterility of his kingdom. One more thing: there is a connection between the shining drinking vessel that comes at the front of the procession, and the Grail procession, and the cauldron of the Welsh poem that is generally considered as one of the prototypes of the Christianized Grail, a magical object that provides an unending source of nourishment but only to those who are deserving, for it pushes cowards away. And it is common knowledge that the hero of the quest must furnish proof of his courage and audacity before successfully reaching his goal.

Nevertheless, Perlesvaus returns to the Grail Castle. He remains there in the company of his mother (who isn't already dead in this version of the story) and his sister. But the two women die. Perlesvaus witnesses the arrival of the ship whose sail is barred by a red cross. He leaves the castle. The Grail now disappears for good and no one can rediscover the path that leads to the unreal Castle of the Four Horns (or Corners). Caer Pedryfan becomes no more than an image in the memory of men. Only a hermit remains at the Grail Castle to perpetuate its memory, but the castle falls into ruin.

This is the tale of *Perlesvaus*. By all the evidence we are dealing with a story written to prove that Glastonbury is the sole place where there is any chance of finding a trace of the Grail, the sole place that can be taken as a departure point for rediscovering the Grail, at least in spirit. But the author made abundant use of traditions that Chrétien de Troyes and his followers didn't wholly retain. The Welsh author of *Peredur* compares more closely to the author of *Perlesvaus*. Should *Perlesvaus*, despite its apparent Christianization, be seen as the most intact remnant of the archetype of the Quest? Perhaps. In any event, this singular work provides an archaic version of the Grail Quest, filled with borrowings from indisputably Celtic traditions of a spirit that is resolutely pagan. Moreover, *Perlesvaus* is another example that sheds light on the fact that the essential framework of the Quest is a story of ritual vengeance through spilled blood.

The *First Continuation* (Pseudo-Wauchier I)

By all the evidence the authors of Chrétien's *Continuations* worked for the court of Flanders. Chrétien himself had undertaken to write *Perceval* for Philip of Flanders. All this seems linked to the famous vial of Precious Blood of Bruges brought from the Holy Land by Philip of Alsace, the count of Flanders. It is also known that stories concerning the miracle of the Precious Blood circulated through the abbey of Fécamp, the preferred monastery of the Plantagenets on the continent, and through Glastonbury. Also supposedly found in Antioch was the lance that had pierced the side of Jesus on the Cross, the lance obviously attributed to a certain centurion Longinius, whose name comes from the Greek name for lance *(lagkias)*. The worship devoted in Flanders and Great Britain to the Precious Blood of Jesus and the Holy Lance found a perfectly natural support in the Grail procession described by Chrétien. The recuperation of the magic lance of the Celts and the mysterious receptacle into Christian symbols was in the natural order of things.

The first text to continue Chrétien's work was attributed for a long time to a certain Wauchier of Denain. In fact the author of the *First Continuation* is unknown. The tale claims to pick up the adventures of Gawain at the point that they are interrupted in Chrétien's work.

Gawain, who had sworn to combat a knight beloved by his sister, returns to keep his promise, but his sister intervenes. Gawain reconciles with his enemy and consents to let the young girl marry him. He departs anew on a series of countless adventures. He promises to reconquer for the Lord of Esclavon a mysterious bleeding lance and gains possession of an ivory horn that strongly resembles the horn that the dwarf enchanter Oberon gave to his protégé Huon of Bordeaux in a contemporary chanson de geste. This horn, in fact, allows him to alert his servants to where he may be located.

A bald and wounded gentleman receives Gawain in the castle. During their meal he sees in procession the Bleeding Lance, the Silver Platter, and the Grail carried by a young girl "who weeps" as well as the coffin in which rests the body of a dead knight. On the knight's chest are two fragments of a sword. Gawain then asks what the Lance and the Grail are, why the girl is weeping, and who the dead knight is. He is answered that he cannot know unless he succeeds in passing the trial of the sword. But he is unsuccessful in putting the two pieces of the sword back together. He goes to sleep and, on the following morning, wakes to find himself in a swamp with his weapons and his horse tied to a tree.

The text seems to follow the archetype quite closely here. The episode of the broken sword is closer to *Peredur* than to *Perceval*, and the same holds true for the detail concerning the weeping bearer of the Grail, which is reminiscent of both *Peredur* and *Jauffré*. It will be noted that it is not enough to ask questions, it is also necessary that the answers be earned. Now, as Gawain is still at a low rank of initiation he cannot claim to know the secret of the Grail.

Gawain pursues his journey and must confront new adventures. Eventually he finds himself again at the Castle of the Grail. The wounded king invites him to dine, and through the Grail's magical intervention the plates refill themselves with marvelous food and the cups with marvelous wine. Gawain again fails in his attempt to join the two sword fragments, but the king announces himself prepared to answer his questions. The Lance is that of Longinius and it will bleed until Judgment Day. The sword has struck an "evil blow" against the dead king in the coffin, which subsequently provoked the withering of the kingdom. But

Gawain, who was tired, falls asleep in the middle of the story and because of that learns nothing about the Grail itself. And he finds himself the next morning on a dune overlooking the ocean.

This second visit of Gawain to the Castle of the Grail thereby denotes another stage in his quest. He is shown the favor of having the secrets unveiled for him but he is incapable of understanding them all and symbolically falls asleep. All he knows now is that he has a mission to accomplish: join together the pieces of the broken sword and avenge the king who died because of it. Here again the theme of ritual vengeance by blood is perfectly clear. What is expected of Grail heroes is not mystical or contemplative attitudes but a bloody deed aimed at regenerating the kingdom. That the bleeding Lance is attributed to the pseudo-Longinius changes nothing of the original theme. Everything would seem to indicate that the author of this continuation utilized the model common to Chrétien and *Peredur's* author. He is satisfied to give a Christian appearance to certain elements that are too pagan to be frankly displayed as such, thus putting his tale in accord with the religious trends of his era. At bottom, all popular authors do the same when they bring an old mythological tale up to date by adorning it with the concerns and motivations of the time, aiming it at a public that will comprehend its contemporary allusions perfectly.

Stranger is the nourishing aspect of the Grail as it appears here. Certainly, in a Christian context it can easily be accepted that the Grail, a sacred vessel—it is not known yet at this point in the story whether it contains the blood of Christ—can procure abundance by consequence of a divine miracle. But this function of the Grail is too close to the function attributed to the sacred cauldron of the pagan Celts to not see it as a resurgence of that myth, which didn't appear in either Chrétien's work, *Peredur*, or *Jauffré*. This cauldron, that "will not provide nourishment to a coward," as seen in the poem by Taliesin already cited, is well known in Welsh mythology. It sometimes appears as an inexhaustible bowl. No group can leave it with their appetite unsated. This anecdote is not Christian but clearly of Celtic provenance and adds yet another mystery to the original Quest theme.

However, Gawain's visit to the Grail Castle hasn't been completely negative. Of course he hasn't achieved the revenge that would have reestablished the previous situation but he has contributed to an improvement of the situation. Indeed, while bemoaning the fact that he missed hearing the end of the wounded king's story, Gawain traverses a landscape that has begun to grow green again. He meets people who give him their blessings for having begun to put an end to the enchantments that weigh over the land. Gawain is therefore an indispensable element for the success of the Quest. He is the precursor, he who opens the way so that the true hero can come forward. The one who, through the achievment of the ritual revenge, delivers the land from the darkness and sterility oppressing it.

But this author of the *First Continuation* stopped his story here.

The *Second Continuation* (Pseudo-Wauchier II)

The author of the *Second Continuation,* who for a long time was also believed to be Wauchier of Denain, doesn't concern himself at all with Gawain's further adventures. It is Perceval who has become the main character. Here again the tests, even though covered with a Christian veneer, seem to derive from the archetype.

Perceval manages to enter a castle that houses a magic horn. He sounds the horn and is forced to battle a knight. The anecdote is almost the same as the episode called "The Joy of the Court" in Chrétien de Troyes's *Erec and Enide.* Perceval defeats the knight and sends him to Arthur's court. While in the castle he sees a chess game that is playing by itself and which checkmates him. Furious he hurls the chessboard through the window, and a young woman emerges from the water to reproach him for this action. He must redeem himself, as in *Peredur,* by returning with the head of a white stag. He succeeds at killing the stag and cutting off its head, but it is stolen from him along with the little dog entrusted to him by the young woman. Through various turns of fortune, and after a short sojourn with his friend Blanchefleur for whom he feels his love growing, he ends by recovering the head and the little dog. He then returns to the castle of the horn, gives the head and the dog to the young woman of the chessboard, and they become reconciled. Furthermore he seems to have totally forgotten Blanchefleur to the benefit of this mysterious "water fairy." This part of the tale is not so different from *Peredur*, proving that this author was also familiar with the common model. But emphasis is placed on the supernatural nature of the young woman with the chessboard. She is obviously a being from the Otherworld, one of the faces of the Empress. And by provoking Perceval she forces him to go beyond himself, to accomplish numerous feats, all the while enjoying with him relations that are ambiguous to say the least and testify, on the one hand, to the pagan origin of the story's basic theme and, on the other, to the convergence of military, magical, sexual, and mystical initiations.

Perceval learns that the chess game was given to the young woman by the fairy Morgan, sister of King Arthur. Thus enters the Grail story this mysterious figure who seems to correspond to the Irish Morrigan, goddess of both war and eros, capable of transforming her appearance into that of a crow, mistress of enchantments, and queen of the Isle of Avalon, the famous Isle of the Apple Trees, the true earthly paradise. The young woman then leads Perceval into a magnificent chamber.

> Perceval didn't fall asleep immediately as was his custom, the young woman's beauty he thought resembled a fairy's. He was thinking this when she came to bed and lay down and acted toward him as he desired and as she had promised. He remained near her without misguided passion as she had sworn a vow to preserve her virginity; they spent the night side by side until morning and the day was clear and beautiful throughout the entire land.*

At first glance the author seems to want to give this scene a reassuring image that conforms to the idea of Perceval as the pure hero who, if not chaste, is nonetheless faithful to his lover Blanchefleur. But this is not the case. Like Peredur, Perceval falls in love with every girl he meets

---

* Simone Hannedouche, trans., *Continuations* (Paris: Éditions Triades, 1968), 131.

during the course of his errantry. In fact, in each instance we are dealing with one of the multiple faces of femininity. And fidelity, in the Celtic conception, is quite different from that preached by Christianity, which again provides additional proof of the tale's Celtic origins. There is, however, something more here, a notion that is akin to a subtle eroticism of which a trace is found among the troubadours and which has often been badly misunderstood.

We are dealing here with an initiatory trial that certain Christian monks, Welsh as well as Irish, practiced for a long while to the great scandal of the zealots of the Roman Church. This trial consisted—for a monk or simply for a holy man—of sleeping in the same bed with a beautiful woman without touching her or having coitus. The goal was to develop carnal ardor and transcend it spiritually, something that it is possible to compare to the rituals of Brahmanic, Buddhist, or Indian tantra. But it also has a connection to fine love (courtly love in other words), the sexual relations between the knight-lover and the mistress-lady, that in the majority of cases consisted of contemplation of the naked body, kisses, caresses, even very extensive ones, sleeping next to one another, all without penetration, which was excluded for motives that were magical as well as moral. Reminiscences of this very specific contemplation of amorous relations can be found in the entire output of the writer—who claimed to be Welsh—John Cowper Powys, but in a morbid and aberrant form. Powys suffered from a certain form of sexual impotence that led him to find his pleasure by sleeping near a young girl, let's say even a very young girl, without touching her, but in idealizing her to the point of idolatry.

In the text of the *Second Continuation*, Perceval is clearly attracted by the young woman of the chessboard. He swears his love to the young woman, embraces her tenderly, and would most likely go much further than that if the girl hadn't set a limit to their game. We are told that she had sworn a vow of virginity. But she hadn't sworn a vow of chastity. She could therefore allow herself to spend the night next to Perceval without the situation leading to coitus. We are told that she had promised Perceval to "provide him pleasure" and that she kept her promise. All is clear. What we are dealing with here, with no room for doubt, is the same type of relationship that was customary in the fine love that was codified and in daily use at the end of the twelfth century and the beginning of the thirteenth. But its mystical and spiritual extension is no less obvious since the young woman of the chessboard is a fairy of the waters, thus a kind of deity. Perceval acquires from his contact with her and the sexual games he enjoys with her a portion of the divine spark that will permit him to pass through the other stages toward the successful resolution of his quest. The young woman of the chessboard remains no less "virgin" in the physical sense of the word. This definitively means that she remains eternally available to aid other men to complete their initiations.

In fact on the following morning the young woman shows Perceval the path that leads to the Castle of the Grail, which is quite significant evidence concerning the value of the sexual trial with which the hero has been confronted. When Wagner in his opera shows us Cundrie the Sorceress—the equivalent of the young girl of the chessboard—in love with Parzival and guiding him toward the Grail, he is only taking up again and sublimating to his own esoteric perspective this scene from the *Second Continuation* that Wolfram von Eschenbach himself had contributed to restoring to its rightful value. In any case eroticism opens a door, whether toward the Other or the Elsewhere, and it would be puerile to deny the importance of this eroticism in the original Quest, especially in a time when these issues constituted a pressing intellectual concern. Wasn't it the troubadour Uc de Saint-Circ who said that one attained God through Woman? This itinerary, which has been— whether one likes it or not—that of the great mystics, is perhaps difficult to understand in our time because eroticism, brutally freed, has become under the name of pornography an object of popular consumption recuperated and commercialized by industrialized neocapitalist society. But at the end of the twelfth and beginning of the thirteenth centuries in western Europe, adherents to the quasi-official trend of thought understood this meaning and its consequences perfectly.

Thus, on the next morning, the young girl of the chessboard conducts Perceval to a ship that, of course, sails without a pilot in conformance with Celtic tradition. She leads Perceval to the other side of a large river and the hero finds himself in a world that is not quite that of humanity. Oddly enough he discovers a man "who was hanging by his feet from a large, thickly leafed oak tree. He was still completely armed and his steed was near him, tied to a branch. The knight was in great pain because he had been hanging for two days" (*Continuations*, 133). We find here the same theme we discovered in Perlesvaus: the ritual sacrifice in honor of the Gallic god Esus.

Perceval takes the knight down and learns that Kay is responsible for the knight's predicament. He sends the knight to Arthur's court where he avenges himself on Kay by knocking him to the ground. Arthur decides that Gawain will go in search of Perceval and the Fisher King in the company of forty knights among whom are Yvain and Lancelot.

As for Perceval, he continues to pursue his journey and enters the Grail Castle. There he is warmly greeted and asked to recount his adventures. While sitting down to dine, Perceval sees the Lance and the Grail carried by a young girl, then a sword in two pieces carried by a valet. Perceval then asks the questions he had neglected to ask on the occasion of his first visit. His host, the wounded king, who is therefore the Fisher King, tells his guest that he will gladly respond on condition that he reunite the two pieces of the sword. Then Perceval "takes the pieces and adjusts the one to the other and the steel knits together as cleanly and beautifully as if it had been done by a smith" (*Continuations*, 152). The king rejoices and declares to Perceval that he can now answer his questions.

But it is precisely at this spot that the *Second Continuation* to Chrétien de Troyes's *Perceval* breaks off its story.

The *Third Continuation* (Manessier)

The author of the *Third Continuation* to Chrétien's *Perceval* is a certain Manessier, who takes the adventures to their logical conclusion, sometimes using the archetype but usually charging the tale with a deliberate intention of Christian recuperation. There is a clear change in the mind-set here and an incontestable antimony exists between Manessier on the one hand and Chrétien and the pseudo-Wauchiers I and II on the other.

We find ourselves again at the Castle of the Grail after Perceval has knit the two pieces of the sword back together. The Fisher King provides explanations to Perceval for all his questions. The Lance is that which Longinius used to stab the side of Christ. The Grail is the vessel that received the blood of Christ after Longinius stabbed him, and it was brought to Great Britain by Joseph of Arimathea. The castle they find themselves in, which bears the name of Corbénic (perhaps meaning "Blessed Court" or "Blessed Cemetery"), was built by Josephus, the nephew of Joseph of Arimathea. The young girl who carried the Silver Platter in the Grail procession is the daughter of Goon of the Desert and is the Fisher King's niece. She who bore the Grail is the king's own daughter. The broken sword is that used by a certain Partinal of the Red Tower to strike a criminal blow against Goon of the Desert, whom he killed, and the Fisher King, whom he wounded. Goon and the Fisher King will only be avenged when the sword has been welded back to-gether by Perceval who must, furthermore, cure the Fisher King by killing Partinal of the Red Tower.

In short we once again find ourselves in the presence of an act of rit-ual blood vengeance. The Grail may well contain the blood of Christ now, yet it is only a secondary object in Perceval's quest whose primary purpose is to avenge and cure the Fisher King in order to restore life and prosperity to a kingdom in full decline. Even though certain medieval-ists have wished to separate this theme of vengeance from that of the Grail at any price it would appear that they are indissolubly linked. Even more it is a family vendetta* as the Fisher King is Perceval's uncle, as was Goon of the Desert.

---

* Contrary to what Jean Marx asserts and repeats in *La Légende arthurienne et le Graal* (Paris: P. U. F., 1952), 335, he hasn't managed to get clear of the "mystical" context of the Quest while he nevertheless recognizes and gives its true value to the Celtic elements of the Quest, elements which at that time were barely accepted by the majority of

And Perceval departs again to complete his mission, exactly like Peredur in the Welsh tale, or Jauffré in the Occitan version. He first undergoes the test of the Chapel of the Black Hand, a cursed location that was the setting for the murder of a woman, who had become a nun, by her own son. The woman's body still remained there and each night a mysterious black hand would appear. To break the spell it would be necessary to take the body and place it outside of the chapel, fight the black hand, then take a white veil out of a cupboard and spread it over the altar after dipping it in holy water, because it is the Devil who is responsible for all this phantasmagoria. Perceval successfully passes this test with no difficulty. This is the point where the Christianization of the text becomes clearly evident; the Devil now makes an appearance in the Quest and this is the first time he has done so. Everything suspect, everything chimerical or magical, everything that doesn't conform to Christian dogma and ritual will now see-saw into the infernal regions. In the early versions of the Quest the supernatural was a neutral presence, neither good nor bad, neither angelic nor demonic, in complete accord with the Celtic mentality that does not accept the concept of sin, that does not accept the concept of the separation of Good and Evil, that does not envision the existence of a Devil who fights against the God of light. There is an influence in Manessier that is not of Celtic origin. Could it be a trace of Catharism? Perhaps. In any case, Manichaeanism was henceforth installed in the Grail Quest, where it would remain, causing the mythological framework of the story to develop toward areas that the first authors, Chrétien de Troyes in particular, had never foreseen.

Furthermore, it is at this point that everything changes in the original

---

medievalists. The great merit of Jean Marx, in this confused work that is full of reversals or errors in the details, is to have sketched out the original outline of the Quest using all available sources as his starting point. This book remains an indispensable tool for whoever wishes to undertake profound research on the Grail, taking into account information contributed since then by literary criticism, archaeology, and the study of Celtic myths.

outline. Perceval is received by a hermit and atones for his sins. The hermit shows him that the kind of life he has been leading to that point will take him to hell for he has not, until the present, used his strength and skill except to kill. This plea for nonviolence, in the middle of a bloody quest, reveals some influence by Cistercian ideas. Henceforth Perceval who, by the nature of things is still required to perform knightly feats, will devote himself to the contemplation of divine mysteries and to protecting himself from all the diabolical attacks that will not fail to occur against him.

Indeed Perceval is now totally engaged with the enemy. In the forest the Devil tries to entice him into the deep water of a river. He is invited by a beautiful young woman—who resembles Blanchefleur—onto a boat that sails there. The young woman gives him much to eat and drink and they end up in a richly adorned bed. Perceval then spies the pommel of his sword in the shape of a cross: he makes the sign of the cross and everything disappears. He sees that the young woman of the boat was the Devil who sought to drag him to his ruin. But, thanks to a gentleman, he finds a boat that can allow him to cross an inaccesible river.

It is then that another young woman, this one angelic, leads him to the smith Trebuchet (called Trébuet in the text). Perceval is sorely in need of his services because his sword is broken and his horse has a nail in one of his hooves. The smith withdraws the nail from the hoof with ease and reforges the sword that he alone has the ability to repair. This episode of the smith plunges us back into the pagan Celtic universe, but it was necessary to include it here so that Manessier could explain the sword episode from Chrétien de Troyes's tale and bring the mysterious Trebuchet into the story.

Perceval again finds Blanchefleur and delivers the Castle of Beaurepaire from her enemies who are once more trying to wrest possession of the young girl's lands. To the great despair of Blanchefleur, who wishes him to stay with her, Perceval takes his leave of her and resumes his quest. In the course of his errantry he meets Hector, the brother of Lancelot of the Lake, and without recognizing him engages him in battle. Both are wounded but cured by an apparition of the Grail.

Hector then leaves in search of Lancelot while Perceval heads toward the castle of Partinal of the Red Tower, a castle that has five towers, one of which is vermilion in color.

Perceval achieves his revenge. He fights for a long while against Partinal and emerges victorious. He does not grant him his life as did Jauffré of Taulat but cuts off his head and brings it back to the Fisher King. When the latter sees the head of his enemy he rises up from his throne. He is cured and his brother Goon of the Desert avenged. He treats Perceval as if he were his own son. It would logically seem that Perceval's quest is now over. It is easy to imagine the hero returning to Blanchefleur and wedding her. The original version of the Quest must indeed have ended with this conclusion but Manessier has substituted a more "mystical" ending. He probably felt that the bloody nature of the Quest didn't conform to the new norms emerging at the heart of contemporary monarchism.

Perceval returns, in fact, to Arthur's court wearing black armor while riding a white horse. This unleashes Kay's sarcasm who declares: "It's the Devil riding an angel from heaven." We are obviously dealing with an image meant to reinforce the Manichaean nature of this later part of the story. King Arthur welcomes Perceval and all the knights returned from the Quest. Each relates his adventures and the king has them written down "in a closet." This provides the opportunity for a festival that lasts eight days. In the minds of Arthur, Perceval, and the other knights the adventures appear to be over.

But just as everyone is enjoying life a maiden arrives on a galloping horse. She is a messenger from the Grail. She announces to the king and to Perceval that the Fisher King has just died. And she specifies that the Fisher King has chosen Perceval to succeed him. It is Arthur himself who crowns Perceval at Corbénic on All Saints' Day, which corresponds exactly to the great pagan Celtic festival of Samhain, a festival for great gatherings and the enthronement of kings. The Grail appears at the table and gives the guests all they could desire by way of food and drink. Here the Grail is even more strongly equated with the Cauldron of Abundance from old Celtic legends. King Arthur and his company remain at Corbénic for a month with Perceval before departing for new feats and adventures.

As for Perceval he reigned at Corbénic for seven years. At the end of this obviously symbolic period of time he entrusted his land to the king of Malone who had married the daughter of the Fisher King, and retired to a hermitage where he was served by the Grail and spent the rest of his life in prayer and meditation. "The day God bore off his soul there was great joy, heaven was enraptured and the Holy Grail and the Lance, and the beautiful silver platter left the earth with him" (*Continuations*, 236). And since that time no one has seen nor will see the Grail and the marvelous objects that disappeared with Perceval.

This edifying end is evidently a creation of Manessier. Nothing in Chrétien's work nor in that of the first two continuators provides any foreshadowing of it. It represents an evolution of the legend and its inflection toward Cistercian mysticism. If elements of the archetype remain in Manessier's continuation, they are buried under different concerns. The Grail has taken its place in the Christian mysticism of the thirteenth century.

The *Fourth Continuation* (Gerbert de Montreuil)

There is, however, a *Fourth Continuation,* or rather another version of the *Third Continuation* that is attributed to the hand of Gerbert de Montreuil, the author of a famous work, the *Roman de la Violette.* The *Fourth Continuation,* which owes nothing to Manessier and most likely was written at a later date around 1225, picks up the Quest at the point where the pseudo-Wauchier II abandoned it.

Despite Perceval's successful passing of the test of the sword, the Fisher King doesn't answer the hero's questions. He instead declares that Perceval is not yet worthy of knowing the secrets of the Grail. It is obvious that the authors have taken greater pains to emphasize the mysterious nature of the Grail. Furthermore, a little later, next to a wall enclosing a marvelous orchard from which Perceval can hear sweet strains of music, he meets an old man who tells him that he can only learn the secrets of the Grail after he has undergone some formidable trials.

Perceval finds himself at Beaurepaire where he sees Blanchefleur again. But Gerbert de Montreuil appears quite embarrassed by Blanchefleur's role in the story, which doesn't exactly conform to Christian morality. This is why Perceval solemnly weds Blanchefleur—just as Parzival will wed Condwiramurs in the German text of Wolfram. It is then prophesied that the descendants of Perceval and Blanchefleur will be illustrious and that they will conquer Jerusalem. Thus the idea of the Crusades finds itself magnified just as is magnified the family of Godefroy de Bouillon for whom Gerbert de Montreuil must have been writing.

But Perceval leaves Blanchefleur to continue his quest. He rewards Gornemant de Goort who had knighted him, and he kills a witch in a combat that is curiously reminiscent of the Welsh *Peredur* text. The author clearly had access to the original model, but only retained its basic elements. Perceval visits the Hermit King who reveals to him that the Grail sustains the Fisher King's life. He delivers the Castle of Montesclaire besieged by a knight whose shield houses a dragon, an episode that recalls a passage from *Perlesvaus*.

He then arrives at an abbey in which he sees, asleep on a bed, a gold-crowned king whose body is covered with wounds. This episode is reminiscent of a passage from *Jauffré*. But in this case the wounded king has not been the victim of a "criminal blow," or a "dolorous stroke" give by a human being; it is God himself that has punished him because he had tried to seat himself at the Table of the Grail without being invited. He is yet a noble figure, a king that valiantly supported Joseph of Arimathea. When he was still a pagan he was named Evallach, but since he was baptized he has been called Mordrach (other later texts call him Mordrain). This name Evallach or Avallach brings us directly back to the myth of the Isle of Avalon whose name in fact means "Apple Trees." Is this the memory of an ancient king of the blessed isle, whose wound—and thus his impotence—caused the withering of the Land of Fairy? Perhaps, but the ancient myth has been largely overlaid by the Christian idea that one cannot receive Communion if one is not in a state of grace.

It is because his heart was not pure and was consequently in a state of mortal sin that King Evallach-Mordrain was punished by God. The same is true for Anfortas, Wolfram von Eschenbach's Fisher King, guilty of having inappropriate sexual relations with the servitors of the Grail. Here the Christianization is even more advanced than in the other *Continuations:* not only is the mysticism clearly visible but morality now has its say.

Perceval learns that this wounded king cannot die—and escape his lengthy suffering—except when a pious knight in quest of the Grail cures him and opens the path of death and pardon. We know this pious knight is Perceval but Gerbert de Montreuil went no further in his tale.

Elucidation

The custom has always been, when a work becomes famous, to compose after the fact a sort of preface that can explain some of the text's obscurities and make clear the meaning that was intended. The quest of Perceval, as seen by Chrétien and the authors of the various *Continuations*, remains somewhat vague and capable of prompting contradictory interpretations. That is why, around the year 1200, an anonymous author thought it wise to propose an elucidation for the entire collection of Perceval stories. Unfortunately he produced a preface-explanation that, in fact, elucidated nothing and contributed to muddying the waters even further. The author's starting point was borrowed, and there is no reason to doubt this, from Celtic sources that are not, however, contained in the archetype text, but for which we have supplied evidence of existence. These were most likely oral sources that would be extremely difficult to pin down. The fact that the author uses a certain Blihis Bliheris as the story's narrator is an argument in favor of this hypothesis. It is, in fact, not hard to see in Blihis Bliheris a historical figure from the middle of the twelfth century who was spoken of by the compiler Giraldus Cambrensis as the *ille famosus fabulator Bledericus.* He was a storyteller *(fabulator)* who was a habitué of the court of Eleanor of Aquitaine in Poitiers and who is considered to have been one of those who familiarized French and Occitan authors with the

Arthurian legends. He may have been either Breton or Welsh, but he knew his subject so well that numerous writers of the end of the twelfth century used his name as a guarantee for their tales' authenticity. He even appeared as a background figure in the *Roman de Tristan* by Thomas, which is an indication that he told this Thomas of England the legend of Tristan. Whatever the case may be, he is the individual, according to the author of the *Elucidation*, that allegedly recounted the adventures preceding the Grail Quest.

Once upon a time in the land of Logres (a Frenchification of the name Lloegr), the term that the Welsh used to designate England proper, but that, in the French romances, is synonymous with Great Britain), there were fairies everywhere who welcomed travelers to mysterious castles. These fairies, who were always very young and beautiful, served travelers like the famous Gallicians of the isle of Sein, according to Pomponius Mela. They supplied them with very white linens, food in abundance and to the personal tastes of the travelers, and marvelous brews in golden cups. But one day a king named Amangon violated one of the fairies and stole the gold cup she used to give drink to travelers. His vassals followed his example. Then a punishment was levied against his kingdom. The lands became barren, the king met a bad end, the trees withered, and the springs dried up. As for the fairies, they disappeared and the road leading to the abode of the Fisher King, the sovereign of this marvelous land, was lost. One of the most characteristic versions of this tale, moreover, deals with another myth, that of the city of Ys, otherwise known as the drowned city. A Welsh poem included in the *Black Book of Carmarthien*, a twelfth-century manuscript, informs us that once there was a town with rich lands around it at the site of the Bay of Cardigan. There was a fountain there guarded by a young girl who watched it to make sure that it didn't overflow. Now one day when he was drunk, a king named Seithenin raped the fountain's guardian and the unwatched fountain started to overflow, inundating the entire surrounding countryside. The same story is repeated in Ireland concerning Lake Neagh (Markale, *L'Épopée celtique d'Irlande*, 39–43). As in the legend of the town of Ys, the theme is the following: a woman guards the waters and keeps watch that they don't overflow, but because of an obstacle—here a rape—the woman no longer watches over the fountain and it overflows. In other words, as consequence of the rape of a fairy by Amangon, the kingdom is sterile, which is the equivalent of a flood in that not only the authors of the rape but all the inhabitants of the land are struck by the punishment.

Thus vanished the Grail, the mysterious castle, and the Fisher King. The narrator, Blihis Bliheris, specifies that the court of the Fisher King perhaps may be found. It would be necessary to search through the forests, and across the moors and lakes until God permitted it to be found. Then joy will be born anew taking the place of the sorrow that hobbles the land. And the Fisher King will once again be found who "very much knows necromancy since he transforms his seeming one hundredfold." He is thus a fairy being comparable to Morgan the Fee, who appears, as does the Empress in *Peredur*, under all the guises he desires to take, thus fooling all those who seek him who are not destined to complete their adventures. But the text concludes by saying that the Fisher King was found again by Gawain.

This strange *Elucidation* informs us very little about the Grail itself, but it has the merit of emphasizing the damage the fairies suffered and the reparation they are due. It is not far from here to the theme of ritual blood vengeance that could well be—in no uncertain terms—the sole and authentic justification of the original Quest. This avenging of the fairies, the guardians of springs and fountains and thus dispensers of fecundity, would therefore be the objective of the Quest. In this way prosperity would be restored to the kingdom. Furthermore it is one of the clearest meanings that can be given to Perceval's adventures, before Christian mysticism distorted the initial outline by insisting on the preeminent role of the Grail. In this *Elucidation*, the "Grail" is truly a magical pagan object, the cup used by one of the fairies to slake the thirst of travelers. This version provides a sketch for the image of the Fisher King's daughter, the bearer of the Grail in the procession described by Chrétien de Troyes. As for the Fisher King: he is a kind of multiform deity who has loomed up from the Celtic pantheon. It is hard to view him as a descendent of Joseph of Arimathea, the guardian of a vessel containing the blood of Christ. When you think that in the most recent versions of the Grail story the Fisher King is named Pellés and that this name is the French equivalent of the Welsh Pwyll "master of the abyss," thus god of the Otherworld, it makes you wonder. . . . Basically, the *Elucidation* is an attempt to restore the legend to its pagan context, a sort of revolt against the Christian recuperation going on in the hands of those authors writing the continuations of Chrétien de Troyes's work. This allows the myth of the inexhaustible bowl or the Cauldron of Abundance to be returned to its rightful place, a magic or divine object that has vanished from the surface of the Earth since a dolorous blow was struck, causing the ruin and sterility of the kingdom. And it goes without saying that only an act of vengeance can restore the previous situation, hence the archaic nature of the Quest, at times masked by Christian motivations, but always presented as being the punishment of a guilty party that entails the healing of the sovereign and the rebirth of the kingdom.

THREE

The Cistercian Grail

Joseph (Robert de Boron)

Robert de Boron's goal was to explain the mysterious container singled out by Chrétien de Troyes and, more importantly, to link it to the Scriptures. To achieve his goals Robert de Boron, an excellent connoisseur of ancient texts, made use of certain passages from the chronicler Grégoire de Tours, passages inspired by the reading of the Apocryphal Gospels and works from various other traditions, particularly the so-called *Acts of Pilate*. The entire first part of his *Joseph* rests, in fact, on these parabiblical assumptions. The second part, which is often confused and full of contradictions, is a talented creation intended to hook the theme of the Grail to these parabiblical elements, all the while making a case for the tenacious tradition that maintains (as Guillaume de Malmesbury asserted) that Great Britain's conversion to Christianity would have started *in valle Avaloniae juxta Glastoniam*, "in the vale of Avalon near Glastonbury." Robert de Boron had no doubts that the abbey of Glastonbury, located on a stony mound in the middle of a swamp, was the site of the fabulous Isle of Avalon, and this is the reason he depicts the Grail as departing for the "Valley of Avaron."

The Grail, which Robert de Boron hadn't yet named as anything other than the "vessel," is the bowl from which Jesus ate during the communal meal on Holy Thursday at Simon the Leper's home. After the death of Jesus, Joseph of Arimathea, a secret disciple of the Savior, came to Pilate to request the crucified body of Christ for burial. It was then that Pilate gave Joseph the vessel. While taking the body down from the cross, Joseph, aided by Nicodemus, saw that the wounds were still bleeding and collected the blood in this vessel.

Later, considered suspect, Joseph was thrown into a dungeon by the Jews and left without food. The resurrected Jesus appeared to him in prison and gave him back this holy vessel. It was thanks to this vessel that he could sustain his life as the sacred object already possessed the power to provide food to those deserving it. De Boron had no difficulty establishing an analogy between this vessel containing the blood of Christ and feeding a persecuted individual, and the Cauldron of Abundance of the ancient Celts. By taking this tradition into account, Robert de Boron was most likely trying to provide a justification for the later Feast of the Grail.

But after the destruction of Jerusalem by the Romans, Joseph is released from prison by the emperors Titus and Vespasian. The relationship Joseph enjoyed with Vespasian was such that he converted the latter to Christianity. Vespasian obtained a boat for him and permitted him to depart toward "faraway lands" in the company of members of the Christian community. Among this community is Joseph's sister, curiously named Enygeüs, whose husband is a certain Bron or Hebron.

The name Bron has inspired much discussion, that of Hebron being most likely biblical in origin, but Bron definitely poses a problem. Is it an abbreviation of Hebron or a Celtic borrowing? In the latter case Bron means "breast, height, eminence, nipple, or hillock," which permits certain commentaries concerning the Grail itself. In addition the name Bron could very well be a variation of Bran who is a well known figure in Welsh mythology, the equivalent of Brennus who captured Rome in 387 B.C. and especially the pseudo-Brennus, hero of the Gallic venture in

Delphi a century later.* This Bran, surnamed Bendigeit (the Blessed) appears in the second branch of the *Mabinogion* as the owner of a strange Cauldron of Resurrection, and his severed head presides over a Feast of Immortality with obvious similarities to the Grail Feast. This Bran also reappears often in the French Arthurian cycle under names such as Brandigan or Bran de Lis (Bran of the Court). He is always a mysterious figure belonging to an undifferentiated Otherworld and endowed with certain magical powers. Sometimes he appears as a giant. But did Robert de Boron truly have knowledge of this mythological figure? We don't have a shred of proof.

Whatever the case may be, Joseph of Arimathea departs aboard his boat toward a faraway Eastern land with a group of Christians, among whom are his sister Enygeüs, his brother-in-law Bron, a logician by the name of Petrus, and a hypocrite named Moys. But sin has slipped into the community. Therefore Joseph, on God's orders, establishes a ritual: the members of the community must join together for a fraternal meal—analogous to that of the first Christians—around a table in the middle of which sits the holy vessel, with a fish caught by King Bron right next to it.

All of this is obviously a recollection of the Last Supper and reveals Robert de Boron's intention to emphasize the divine presence, according to the theological trends of his era. The fish is, of course, the Greek *Icthus,* which serves as a symbol for Jesus and was a rallying sign for the first Christians. But it also allows the author to establish a link between Bron and Chrétien de Troyes's Fisher King.

Joseph lays down precise rules concerning this feast of the holy vessel. Only those touched by the grace of God are admitted to this table, on which rests the problem so often debated by Pelagius and Saint Augustine concerning the help given by God to certain human beings so that they may find salvation. The guests admitted to this table experience an indescribable joy, which is the ecstatic exaltation obtained from receiving Communion, quite in the tone of Cistercian theology. Those

* See Jean Markale, *The Celts* (Rochester, Vt.: Inner Traditions, 1993), 66–80.

not welcome at this table are therefore reprobates, people who God doesn't deign to touch with his grace. And these individuals understand nothing of what is taking place there. Robert de Boron seems to foresee Perceval's first visit to the Castle of the Grail, as well as Gawain's and Lancelot's visits. In addition, there is an unoccupied seat in this assembly that prefigures the Round Table instituted by Merlin. This is the seat of Judas that would subsequently become the Perilous Seat. No one should sit there except the person predestined to bring the adventures to an end. The hypocrite Moys had the audacity to sit in it and was swallowed up by the earth. This feast takes place every day allowing the guests to be nourished spiritually and materially according to their desires and capabilities. Robert de Boron calls this the "Service of the Grail," for from this point on the holy vessel is named the Grail, "because it suits all those who see it" (verse 2659). The etymology is quite within the taste of the time.

Additionally a divine voice makes itself heard and reveals the magic power of the Grail: those admitted into the service of the Grail will be spared any unjust ruling in a court of law. They cannot be wounded in their limbs, nor be betrayed in their right, nor defeated in battle (verses 3049–52). They are under God's protection. A secret teaching is attached to the Grail. These are the "sweet and precious words" that are only known by the master of the Grail, which brings to mind the secret prayer revealed to Perceval by the Hermit King in Chrétien de Troyes's story. Thus, thanks to Robert de Boron, the secret and esoteric nature of the Grail is emphasized, and it is henceforth absolutely inaccessible to common men, reserved exclusively for those who deserve the knowledge, those who have achieved the slow initiation that leads to the discovery of the holy object. The original Grail, in passing from one author to another, has gone from a simple container holding an unspecified content to an object of the highest virtue, the crystal that converges all the rays that are the desires of humanity. Consequently the Quest will no longer be a matter of family vengeance but one of an individual asceticism destined for the acquisition of a perfect knowledge.

After establishing this "Service of the Grail," Joseph of Arimathea entrusted the Grail and confided its secret to his brother-in-law Bron who henceforth "by his right name be called the Rich Fisherman." Chrétien de Troyes had spoken of the Fisher King because this wounded and impotent individual spent his time fishing on a lake. Robert de Boron charges the character with a symbolic function: he fishes for God represented by the Fish. And in other texts he will take on the image of God fishing for men so that they may be saved.

Joseph of Arimathea remains in the Orient where he will soon die. Bron and his twelve sons depart "toward the West." One of these sons, Alain, a typically Celtic name, will be the master architect of the Christian conversion of these lands and the father of the Grail King lineage. Later, Petrus, who had remained with Joseph of Arimathea, has a revelation. He must leave to rejoin Bron and Alain "in the land toward the West that is harshly savage." And one learns at the same time the name of the place he must go: "To the Valley of Avaron I will go, there by his grace God will await" (verses 3221–22). There, as stated in the prose composition that follows from Robert de Boron's poem, "he halted to await the son of Alain, and could not go from life to death before he had read the message to him and taught and spoke of the strength of your vessel, and he who will come will give news of you."*

So ends Robert de Boron's *Joseph;* the link between the legend of Joseph of Arimathea and Perceval's quest is now solidly established. Everything is in place for the later development of the legend and its essentially mystic character.

The Didot-Perceval (Robert de Boron)

In Robert de Boron's *Merlin,* the author incorporates this semihistorical, semilegendary character into the Arthurian context and places in the mouth of the enchanter-prophet a veritable summary of his book *Joseph.* Merlin, before King Arthur and all his knights, ends a speech with these words:

Le Roman du Graal (Paris: Éditions 10/18, 1981), 66.

The Fisher King remains in these Irish isles in one of the most beautiful places of the world. And know that he is in the direst of circumstances that ever a man was in, and that he has succumbed to a great illness. But I can clearly tell you this much, that, whatever his age and infirmity he can only die when a knight who will be of the Round Table has performed so many feats of arms and chivalry in tournament and by the seeking of adventures that he will be the most renowned throughout the world. And that knight, when he has been so exalted that he will be able to go to the court of the Fisher King and when he will have asked what the Grail has served and what it is it serves, then immediately the Fisher King will be cured. And he will unveil to him the sacred words of Our Lord and then depart this life. And this knight will have the blood of Jesus Christ in his keeping. Then the enchantment will fall from the land of Britain and the prophecy will be fulfilled. (*Roman du Graal*, 194–95)

It will be noted that there is no longer any mention of the Bleeding Lance, the Silver Platter, the sorrow of the guests, or the sword broken into two pieces. Attention is drawn uniquely to the Grail and the mission of the knight to come as the keeper of the Precious Blood. This is the theme developed by Robert de Boron in his *Didot-Perceval*, so named for the name of one of the manuscript's owners and to differentiate it from Chrétien de Troyes's *Perceval*. This work, of which all that remains for us is an early thirteenth-century prose adaptation, is in some respect the synthesis of everything written until then on the quest of Perceval the Welshman.

Shortly before his death, Perceval's father, named Alain li Gros, is warned by the Holy Ghost that his son is destined to become king of the Grail. He advises the young man to go to Arthur's court and be knighted. This Perceval does at his father's death. He is knighted by Arthur himself and participates in the Pentecostal feast, where, on Merlin's advice, the restoration of the Round Table is begun. Perceval covers himself with glory from various tournaments. There is at the Round Table a "perilous seat" on which no one sits because Merlin has said it was reserved for one of heaven's choosing and the imprudent who dared sit in it would be annihilated. Perceval claims the honor of sitting there. Arthur begins by refusing, but, following Gawain's entreaties, relents and allows Perceval's request. Perceval seats himself. At this moment the stone upon which the seat was built splits, a shout comes out of the earth, and night falls on the surrounding area. A voice then reproaches Arthur for having permitted this transgression as consequence of which King Bron, the Fisher King (in other words Perceval's grandfather) has just fallen into a state of great infirmity. King Bron can only be healed and the stone joined together again when one of the knights seated at the table has surpassed all others in valor, succeeded in discovering the path to the Castle of the Grail, and asked the necessary questions about the Grail.

This beginning of the *Didot-Perceval* calls for much commentary. First of all it is quite possible that, in the author's mind, Perceval's father could be the famous Alain li Gros of *Joseph*, since King Bron is the hero's grandfather. In any case, as with Chrétien de Troyes, *Peredur's* author, and the author of *Perlesvaus*, the quest is a family matter, Perceval being the nephew or grandson of the Fisher King. By birth he is a member of the family of Grail guardians.

The theme of the Perilous Seat was already sketched out in *Joseph*, with a reference to the role of Judas and the punishment of the hypocrite Moys who sat on the forbidden seat during the "Grail Service." Now the anecdote relayed in the *Didot-Perceval* goes way beyond a simple story of a chair cursed because of the memory of the traitor Judas. This is unquestionably a Celtic theme. Indeed the adventure recounted here is fairly similar to the enthronement rite for the overking of Ireland in Tara, according to the epic tale *The Race of Conaire the Great*:

> At Tara there were two blocks of stone that could be opened. But they could only be opened by the one who was worthy to hold the throne of Tara. And then there was the Fal Stone: when a man was worthy of holding the throne of Tara, it shouted, and in such a way that all could hear it. (Markale, *L'Épopée celtique d'Irlande*, 176)

On this point there can be no coincidence; it is a deliberate borrowing from Irish tradition. The Celtic ritual of royal enthronement supposes a magical or divine intervention: the predestined individual was recognized by nature and the deity, thus the stone shouted out beneath him when the two blocks were separated. In the *Didot-Perceval* where the circumstances are not identical, it is the stone that serves as the foundation of the chair that splits (thus separates) and cries out. As we know Perceval is destined to become the king of the Grail, we understand quite well that we are concerned here with a ritual of royal enthronement in the Celtic style, something perfectly normal in the context of the Celtic framework of the Arthurian world.

But what is strange is that this incident is perceived by the author as sacrilegious. Perceval didn't yet have the right to sit on the Perilous Seat, hence the culpable nature of the act and the infirmity of the Fisher King considered as a family punishment. In any case Perceval wasn't struck by lightning or swallowed up by the earth, which shows that he is worthy, under certain conditions, of occupying this seat. It would seem that Robert de Boron—or his adapter—wanted to return to the original outline of the Quest, that is to say, to the revenge-reparation performed by a nephew, or a grandson, to cure the sick king and thus the barren kingdom.

But this assumes that Robert de Boron didn't comprehend this ritual of royal enthronement. On the other hand, the second part of Robert de Boron's *Merlin*, a second part that is moreover more recent than the first and improperly placed under Robert's warranty, provides another explanation for the Fisher King's infirmity. In truth, the very text, in the two manuscripts that have been preserved, is truncated at this spot and contains only the beginning and end of this episode. But the rest can be supplied by the English compilation of Thomas Malory, *Le Morte d'Arthur*, or by *Le Roman de Balaain*, an episodic work of the thirteenth century.* According to this version that is, let me repeat, placed under the patronage of Robert de Boron, the Fisher King's infirmity is caused

---

*D. Legge, ed., *Le Roman de Balaain* (Manchester: 1942).

not by Perceval or one of his failings, but by a "dolorous blow" that he fell victim to following some unfortunate circumstances. Indeed the knight Balin, or Balaain, of Arthur's court has emerged successfully from a test that allowed him to acquire a somewhat magical sword. Merlin warns him that this Sword of the Strange Belt will strike the "dolorous blow" that will plunge three kingdoms into mourning and misery. Balin doesn't heed Merlin's advice. As his adventures proceed we find him at the castle of King Pellehan, that is to say, Pellés, the Fisher King, where he must avenge a series of murders committed by Pellehan's own brother, a certain Garlan (probably the same character as the renegade brother of Pellés, master of Castle Mortal in *Perlesvaus*). Balin kills him. Pellehan then pursues his brother's murderer who seeks refuge in a magnificent chamber. On a table there is an upside-down Lance that seems to be miraculously held over a gold basin. Balin seizes the Lance and strikes Pellehan with it. The castle collapses. A voice announces that the Lance has been touched by unworthy hands and that "the adventures are going to begin." Merlin arrives to save Balin, who will nevertheless die a little later on with Merlin unable to protect him.* There is a great deal of incoherence in all of this since the "dolorous blow" is not stuck with a sword but the Lance. It is true that this Lance closely resembles the one portrayed by Chrétien de Troyes in the Grail procession.

It is obvious that Robert de Boron—or his continuator—has blended two different traditions here. Both are Celtic, however. The first emphasizes the enthronement of the king of the Grail when the stone cries out and splits in two. The second makes use of the original outline of the Quest by favoring the theme of blood vengeance that should bring healing to the Fisher King. But it is very likely that the first tradition concerning enthronement corresponds more to the overall plan Robert de Boron had for his work, one in keeping with the author's desire that the vengeance theme be forgotten in favor of one concerning the mystical royalty of the Grail, a royalty that allows access to the

---

* Emmanuele Baumgartner, trans. *Merlin le Prophète*, (Paris: Éditions Stock Plus, 1980), 223–73.

highest form of knowledge, that of the great secrets of the Grail.

Whatever the case may be, the stone of the Perilous Seat is split and everyone knows it will only be reunited when one of the knights of the Round Table has completed a quest. All the knights present, of course, decide to depart, convinced they will be successful. And Perceval, as in the Welsh story and the novel by Chrétien, swears he will not spend two consecutive nights in one place until he has found the Castle of Wonders. King Arthur, somewhat sadly, witnesses the departure of all his knights.

Perceval is the hero of numerous adventures. He must fight a giant. Then the well-known episode of the magic chessboard and the hunt of the white stag takes place. After having brought back the head of the stag he meets his sister who informs him of his mother's death, but in this version of the legend it is not his fault that she has died, as is the case in Chrétien de Troyes's version, and Perceval is not at fault for leaving the maternal domain. Merlin appears to him as a woodchopper and offers him some advice. Basically, he reminds him to ask the questions relating to the Grail if he wants to heal the Fisher King. Merlin thus intervenes in Perceval's quest as both a guide and a counselor: the enchanter-prophet knows the turns and detours of the labyrinth whose heart holds the Grail, but though he is not stingy with advice, he still refrains from organizing anything, leaving all their freedom of choice and decision. It seems there is still a Cistercian influence here; the problem of grace arose again around the year 1200 and soon led to the Thomist formulation, a compromise between Augustinism (one cannot find salvation save through the grace of God, which he only grants to those he has chosen) and Pelagianism (absolute free will, one can be saved if one chooses to be saved with no need of the grace of God). In sum, Merlin's intervention is the equivalent of the grace of God, necessary for finding the path leading to illumination, but this grace is only an aid; the human being has complete freedom to either benefit from it or refuse it.

Indeed Perceval enters the Castle of the Grail, but when confronted by the famous procession described so many times by the various authors, he remembers his mother's advice concerning the discretion and humility to be observed under all circumstances and doesn't dare to ask the long-awaited questions. On the next day when he wakes the castle is empty, as if no one had ever lived there. His horse is completely saddled in the stable and he leaves. He is subject to the reproaches of a young maiden who weeps because he hasn't passed his test and he wanders for seven years, a symbolic figure of course, in despair at having failed his mission.

He ends by finding his uncle, the Hermit King, again. He learns of his sister's death and pays penitence for two months. Merlin appears to him still in his guise as a woodchopper and leads him to the Grail Castle. One has the impression that the author intentionally accentuated Merlin's role in order to quash the more dubious and ambiguous role of the damsels that guided the hero of the original Quest, mainly in the Welsh *Peredur*. This tendency to minimize the role of women in the Quest reveals a profound monastic influence. It was necessary to remove both all ideas of sexuality and all references to the latent paganism still embodied in these female figures of fairylike appearance.

Perceval is therefore received by the rich Fisher King. He takes part in the feast: "And as the first comestibles were brought to the table, a Lance emerged from a chamber, bleeding from its tip, and after came the Grail, and the maiden who bore the small silver Platter." Perceval then asked the purpose of what he was seeing. He had hardly spoken when "the Fisher King was cured of his illness and as healthy as a fish." It will be noted that he had no need to cure the king with any sort of deed or secret: it was enough to ask the question. It was the word that healed and restored the previous situation, the magical word that one was awaiting that allowed the connection between what was and what will be. It is at heart a shamanic action Perceval achieves here, and the episode conforms to the outline of numerous folktales in which the hero, abruptly plunged into a mysterious city belonging to the Otherworld, restores life to that city by asking a question, starting a dialogue, or by buying something. In the extreme, one could ask if the Grail was really necessary in all this. It is not the Grail, or even the Lance, that heals, as will be the case in the later *Quest of the Holy Grail*, it is Perceval's intervention. In reality, the tale of the *Didot-Perceval*, despite its monastic influences and deliberate mystical bias, remains quite close, at least in this episode, to the original Quest, and likewise in *Perlesvaus*, the Fisher King is cured simply by seeing the head of his enemy carried by the hero.

However, the Fisher King reveals the secrets of the Grail to Perceval. The holy vessel is the one that caught the blood of Christ, and the Lance is that of Longinius who stabbed Jesus in the side. The Fisher King kneels before Perceval and entrusts him with the royalty of the Grail. He dies three days later. At the same moment at Arthur's court, where all the knights returned from the Quest have gathered, there is a terrible noise and the stone of Perilous Seat fuses together. Thus both Perceval's royalty and the royal enthronement function of the Perilous Seat are both confirmed, all is restored to order, and the stone that cries out and splits is ready for a new trial when the problem of Perceval's succession arises. As for Merlin, he immediately returns to the Castle of the Grail in the company of his friend and master, the hermit Blayse, who moreover supposedly relayed this story under Merlin's dictation.

It must be said that Blayse remains an enigma. Why did Robert de Boron introduce such a character? The name Blayse (Blaise in French) is a clumsy but practical Frenchification of a Welsh word (Bleidd) and Breton word (Bleiz) that mean wolf. In Geoffroy of Monmouth's *Vita Merlini*, we learn that Merlin spent a part of the year in a house that permitted observation of the stars, and the other part in the woods in the company of a gray wolf. Merlin is the man of the woods who knows the language of wild animals, of which the wolf is the most characteristic representative.* There are obvious traces here of traditions concerning an ancient shamanic-style religion. Merlin and Blayse form the Man-Animal couple reconstituting primordial times. They are the witnesses of the regeneration of the Grail kingdom, that is to say, the reconstitution of the edenic universe that existed at the dawn of time.

Thus end the spells weighing on Britain. But Arthur's troubles are not

---

*See Jean Markale, *Merlin: Priest of Nature* (Rochester, Vt.: Inner Traditions, 1995), 164–69, and *L'Épopée celtique en Bretagne*, 119.

over. A part of the tale, which will be subsequently more fully developed in *La Mort d'Arthur*, in the last section of the *Prose Lancelot*, concerns the strife between Arthur and his nephew Mordred who has usurped power in the king's absence. Arthur and Mordred fight one another, according to the outline put forth by Geoffroy of Monmouth in his *Historia Regum Britanniae*. Mordred is killed. Arthur is fatally wounded but is brought by his sister, Morgan the Fee, to the Isle of Avalon from which he will one day be resurrected to unite all of Britain. As for Perceval who has become king of the Grail, he spends his days praying for his friends of the Round Table, which exists no more. Merlin, still accompanied by Blayse, has a dwelling built not far from the Castle of the Grail. This is where he dictates the tale of the Grail to Blayse and also where he speaks all the prophesies that God has commanded him to say.

This text of the *Didot-Perceval* is of extreme importance. It constitutes a synthesis between the different traditions concerning the Grail. It integrates the original version of the Quest into a more clearly Arthurian context, all the while developing the spiritualist concepts of the Cistercians. It establishes the connection between those elements that are foreign to the original Quest and the framework itself, all while respecting the Arthurian outline proposed by the literary introducer of the cycle, Geoffroy of Monmouth. Henceforth the entire Arthurian adventure will be marked, in one way or another, by the Grail and by the Quest that must be accomplished toward the castle that guards this "so holy thing." And, to a certain extent, the Quest, by its vicissitudes and unexpected extensions, will be one of the causes for the destabilization, then collapse, of the Arthurian world. It is in the nature of things since, in the last analysis, the chivalrous adventures are but folly and vanity with respect to the spiritual quest, the only one that can bring the soul to the threshold of the divine.

The *Estoire du Saint Graal*

It was around the years 1220–1230 that the prose romances, forming what are called either the *Prose Lancelot*, the *Corpus Lancelot-Grail*, or the *Vulgate* (if using the title given it by the lone editor of this vast grouping, Oskar Sommer), were written by different authors hiding behind the authority of one Walter Map, a thirteenth-century Latinized writer from England. The entire Arthurian legend, up to its final stages, is contained herein and the Grail holds a particular place of honor.

The first of these romances, which incidentally is not the oldest, is *Estoire du Saint Graal*: this text serves as a sort of preface to the Arthurian texts as well as their justification. The author takes Robert de Boron's *Joseph* and develops it further, striving to accentuate the mystical signification of the Grail to an even greater degree. The work is presented as a "vision." It is God himself that dictated everything to the narrator during a long ecstatic trance in which the author's soul was transported to heaven.

The beginning conforms to Robert de Boron's text. The Grail is the bowl in which Joseph of Arimathea gathered the blood of Christ during the crucifixion. The lone innovation is that Joseph has a son named Josephus, the first ordained priest and bishop: this detail reveals the extent to which the author sought to integrate the Grail legend into a sacerdotal context. Furthermore, the "Service of the Grail" becomes more and more identical to the celebration of the sacrifice of the Mass; angels bring Joseph the Holy Oil that has since "served to consecrate the kings of Great Britain." It is evident that the sarcedotal tendency is not in conflict with a smart political maneuver that seeks to portray the Plantagenets as sovereigns legitimized by long tradition and holy unction, identical to the kings of France. In any case it is the proof that the author is, if not English, at least in the circle of influence of John Lackland. And when Josephus celebrates the Grail Mass, those who take communion see the bread in the form of a "fully grown child."

There are new details. Accordingly, Josephus is wounded in the thigh by an angel—as the Fisher King will be—with a blow from the sacred Lance, because he momentarily left a baptism ceremony to exorcise some demons. However, in the Holy Land, Joseph converts the pagan kings Evallach and Serapha who take the names of Nascien and Mordrain, and who make a prophecy concerning the identity of those who will be in the lineage of Holy Grail guardians. Joseph and his companions leave to traverse the Celtic countries and establish themselves somewhere on the isle of Britain. King Mordrain draws too close to the Grail without having the requisite purity: he loses his sight, which means that he couldn't see the "high secrets" the Grail supposedly holds, or that he couldn't tolerate the dazzlement the knowledge of these secrets caused. He can only be cured of this blindness by a "Good Knight," issued from the Grail lineage, one who has completed his adventures.

On a mysterious Turning Island, King Evallach-Nascien discovers a boat that sails without a pilot. This is the ship of King Solomon. On board this ship a Sword of the Strange Belt is found, in other words a sword in an extraordinary baldric. Evallach-Nascien takes this sword that may only be drawn from its scabbard by the "Good Knight" who will bring these adventures to their just conclusion.

This entire episode plunges us back into the most ancient of Celtic mythology. The Turning Isle is well known to Irish authors who described the fabulous voyages in search of the Land of Fairy, the island the Irish call Emain Ablach, the famous isle of apple trees called Avallach, that is to say, Avalon, by the Welsh. And it is not by chance that the discovery of this island, ship, and sword is due to Evallach whose name is obviously the same as Avallach. Furthermore the theme of the boat without a pilot is quite widespread in stories of Celtic origin; as for the sword that only the predestined hero can pull from its scabbard, this is a recollection of Kaledfwlc'h, the sword of King Arthur that can only be drawn out of its magic stone by the king whom God has chosen. This is again a royal enthronement ritual of the Celtic world.

It is thanks to the boat of Solomon that Joseph and his companions preached the Gospel throughout Great Britain. Bron, Joseph's brother-in-law, and his twelfth son Alain li Gros, founded the lineage of Grail guardians. The fisherman Moys, who wanted to sit in the forbidden place during a Grail repast, was swallowed by flames. One day when the table was lacking in food, Alain li Gros caught an enormous fish in a pond. When pieces were cut from the flesh of this fish they multiplied miraculously. It was from this point on that he gained the name of the Rich Fisherman.

After the deaths of Joseph and Josephus, Alain li Gros, the Fisher King and titular guardian of the Grail, had the Castle of Corbénic built to house this sacred relic. This castle is "adventurous," that is to say, those who risk its adventures uninvited put their lives at stake. King Lambor, one of Alain's successors, engages in war against a certain King Brulan (who is none other than the Balin from the story of Merlin), who strikes him a blow with the Sword of the Strange Belt. This is Britain's first dolorous blow: it entails war and devastation, the wheat doesn't germinate, the trees become barren, the fish disappear from the waters. And this land is called the Waste Land. As for the son of Lambor, Pellehan, (Pellés in other words), he is *méhaigné,* that is to say, wounded in the course of a battle. Only the "Good Knight" can cure the kings who are "maimed" and restore fecundity to the Waste Land.

Thus, with this *Estoire du Graal* whose framework, drawn from Robert de Boron, bears the imprint of various influences, the setting of the great Arthurian epic is henceforth in place. All that is still lacking are the heroes to perform the adventures.

The *Lancelot Proper*

This extremely long romance, the oldest in the series, although forming its third part (the second being an adaptation of Robert de Boron's *Merlin*), is a sort of corpus of Arthurian adventures drawn from a wide array of sources. The stories feature Lancelot of the Lake as their main character, whose legend, before Chrétien de Troyes, was completely foreign to the Arthurian cycle. Only some of its episodes concern the Grail.

Since Merlin's founding of the Round Table, to which only five hundred knights can gain admittance—and that's including the famed Perilous Seat—all of Arthur's knights have regularly left in quest of adventure and returned to court to recount what they have done. One day Gawain, the king's nephew, enters Corbénic where he is received by the Fisher King, who invites him to dine. The Grail procession passes through the room. Everyone falls to their knees, but Gawain, dazzled by the beauty of the young girl bearing the Grail, has eyes for her alone. When the Grail passes by the tables they become filled "with all the good meats and all the good smells." But in front of Gawain there is nothing. When the meal ends all the guests disappear. Gawain goes to sleep. But during the night he is wounded by a lance. He witnesses combats between fantasy beasts, sounds of lamentation fill the air, and he must fight a knight in a combat that ends at a draw. The young girl holding the Grail makes her reappearance at this juncture. Gawain is healed of his wounds, but carried off by a crowd of people who place him in a cart. He is dragged through a city where all the inhabitants hiss and boo him. Later he meets a hermit who explains to him that he had been in the presence of the holy "vessel" that contained the blood of Christ and through ignorance had not recognized it. And the hermit adds that the Grail is not for sinners who don't repent, no matter their prowess nor what deeds they have achieved.

Gawain's bungled test provides a faithful depiction of the state of mind of the Cistercian Quest. Gawain is brave and valorous but he has one defect: he is overly sensual. He only had eyes for the young girl carrying the holy vessel and not for the vessel itself. Hence his failure and shame. In the author's mind, and this will be repeated on many occasions, the one who overcomes the tests of the Grail can only be a man of untainted purity, truly virginal and chaste. Thus comes to light an idea that didn't appear in the outline of the original Quest in which Perceval-Peredur was hardly a model of virtue according to that century's Christian standards. The Quest is thus entirely emptied of the magical-sexual components that unquestionably existed in the original Celtic archetype.

It is Lancelot of the Lake's turn to be faced with the test. In the course of his numerous adventures he meets a beautiful woman who gives him lodging and takes him to the Castle of Corbénic the following day. Lancelot succeeds at a test that Gawain failed at: he pulls a young girl from a tub of boiling water into which she had been plunged up to her waist. Then he raises up the flagstone of a tomb on which is written "This tombstone will not be lifted until the return of the leopard from whom the great lion will emerge. The leopard will lift it and the lion will be engendered upon the beautiful daughter of the king of Foreign Land."* Lancelot also kills a horrible serpent that comes out of the tomb.

Of course the hero doesn't comprehend the meaning of this prophesy. He doesn't yet know that he is the leopard who will give birth to the great lion, his son Galahad. He is welcomed by Pellés the rich Fisher King and is a witness to the Grail procession. But, in contrast to Gawain, he kneels and clasps his hands in prayer when the young girl holding the richest "vessel" that ever was seen by mortal man and "similar to a chalice" goes by. Lancelot finds excellent food before him, exactly like the other guests.

Lancelot, however, is not the chosen one. He bears a serious sin, for he committed adultery with Queen Guinivere whom he loves with a mad passion that is so exclusive he never looks at any other woman. Now Pellés knows that the adventures of the Grail will be completed by a "Good Knight" who is an issue from both Lancelot of the Lake—the best knight in the world—and someone of the Grail lineage. With the complicity of Brisane, the wet nurse/lady-in-waiting of his daughter Elaine, the bearer of the Grail, he contrives a strange plan to make Lancelot sleep with Elaine. Certainly there is a precedent for this in the original Arthurian cycle. Arthur was born as a result of the shameful relations between Uther Pendragon and Queen Ygern, Uther having been enchanted in such a way by Merlin that he had taken on the appearance of Ygern's husband. The theme is the same here. The predestined knight must not only have an extraordinary birth, but even a conception that is out of the ordinary. It could be said that all of this hardly conforms to the virtuous spirit of the Cistercian Quest. But the birth of Jesus Christ, after all, is ambiguous, to say the least, and as the Good Knight will be in the image of Christ, his conception can and must be made in exceptional circumstances.

*Oskar Sommer, ed. *Prose Lancelot,* vol. 3 (Washington, D. C.: Carnegie Institute, 1909), 104.

The problem is that Lancelot is desperately faithful to Guinivere. There is nothing in the world for which he would betray his queen. So, the lady-in-waiting Brisane enters the game. Brisane bears a great resemblance to the lady-in-waiting Luned of Chrétien de Troyes's *Chevalier au Lion*, and furthermore, we are told she is one of the companions of Lancelot's adoptive mother, Vivian, the Lady of the Lake. She is a fairy and a magician. Thanks to a philter for which she knows the secret, Lancelot (who is in an altered state) is convinced that he will be reuniting with Queen Guinivere when it is with Elaine that he will be sharing his bed. This is how the future Galahad, the "Good Knight" that had been so long awaited, was engendered on that night from the daughter of the Fisher King and the best knight in the world.

On waking Lancelot is furious at having been deceived in this way and having involuntarily cheated on the queen. But he ends by excusing Elaine, takes his leave of the Fisher King, and finds himself caught up in a series of fantastic adventures, one in particular that is a sort of eternal ball that he does, however, contribute to ending. After numerous exploits and trials, wounded and confused, Lancelot returns to Corbénic. He is recognized by the king's daughter who heals him with the Grail. It is then that he learns he has a son and this son's name is Galahad.* It is also at Corbénic that he is rejoined by his brother Hector and by Perceval who is pursuing a solitary quest. Perceval tells Lancelot that the queen requests his presence at court. Lancelot takes Galahad

---

* Lancelot's baptismal name was in fact Galahad, a name given him by his father King Ban of Benoïc. It was the Lady of the Lake (Vivian), who had kidnapped him to raise him in her fairy castle, that gave him the cognomen of Lancelot of the Lake. Numerous researchers have thought this name to have some relationship with the name of the Irish god Lugh, surnamed Lamfada, meaning "long spear." Lancelot of the Lake would therefore be a clumsy transposition of Lugh Lamfada by way of its Welsh form Llwch Llyminawc, that doesn't occur in some texts, in particular the tale of *Culwch and Olwen* and a poem attributed to Taliesin. It should be noted that Lancelot of the Lake never appears in ancient Welsh tradition before the thirteenth century, and in this instance he has his French name. But this does not exclude the existence of an equivalent mythological figure.

with him, whom he has reared in an abbey close to Camelot, and returns to Arthur and Guinivere's presence. This episode of *Lancelot* marks a decisive turning point in the evolution of the Quest, a turning point that won't even appear in the Germano-Iranian tradition of Wolfram von Eschenbach. The Grail hero will no longer be Perceval, but a newcomer entirely fabricated—this is the occasion to say so—for the needs of the cause. Perceval was definitely too suspect of unacceptable pagan legacies and couldn't be used in the sacerdotal and mystical framework of the Cistercian Quest. Though Perceval was a valiant knight, he was overly blemished by stains and weaknesses. As the Grail was an "object so holy" that impure hands could not touch it without risking disaster, it was necessary to create a special hero, the ideal priest as imagined by the Cistercians who were obsessed with sanctity and purity. In creating Galahad, the model of the priest was created, even though this model is too good to be true. The creation of this priestly model singularly weakened the range of the Quest. In place of a slow period of initiation, instead of a long and painful wandering of the soul through the various dangers, strayings, and snares of life, the Quest has become a simple stroll achieved by a superman. When all is said and done, the Grail has been made inaccessible to humans, even though these same humans would have desired with all their hearts and strength this sublime epilogue that constitutes the great secrets of the Grail.

This also causes certain questions to be raised concerning the name of the predestined hero. At first glance the name Galahad presents no problems. It is of biblical origin and connected to the tribe of the same name. In reality the problem is not that simple. We find ourselves unquestionably in a Celtic context and the names from the Arthurian epic that belong to Celtic tradition are numerous. Evallach is related to the Isle of Avalon. Pellés is Pwyll, master of the abyss of Welsh tradition. Lancelot is perhaps the god Lugh, humanized and given a historical context. Gawain-Gwalchmei is a deity of the solar variety. Arthur is the Bear God. Guinivere is the Mother Goddess. Morgan is a goddess of warrior-eros. Vivian is a goddess of the waters. Merlin, son of a devil and a female saint, is the image of the Demiurge. Peredur-Perceval is one of the aspects of the Young Son that will restore life to a barren kingdom. Why wouldn't Galahad belong to this lineage of gods and heroes transposed by the needs of the time, even if his creation is justified in the Cistercian perspective of that moment?

There is no proof that Galahad's name comes from the Bible. Its appearance in both contexts could simply be a chance encounter. Indeed the root of the name can be considered as a Celtic Gal or Galu, that occurs in Britannic languages as meaning both "stranger" and "strong, powerful." According to the story of *The Quest of the Holy Grail*, Galahad is invincible, he goes right to his goal, he commits no errors like Perceval, he undoes all the malefic spells that oppose the success of his mission, he always defeats his enemies, and frees all those who are oppressed. He is truly *powerful.* This is only a hypothesis but it is impossible to disregard it if one wishes to act in good faith. Because to vanquish the Darkness, purity and light are not incompatible with Power, as is proven by the myth of Apollo trampling the serpent Python, a myth transposed into Christianity in the appearance of Saint Michael defeating the dragon.

The Quest of the Holy Grail (Walter Map)

Étienne Gilson has done a remarkable job of shedding light on the specific nature of *The Quest of the Holy Grail* in an article entitled "The Mysticism of Grace."* Using as his starting point the considerations of the medievalist Albert Pauphilet concerning the incontestable influence of the Cistercian Order on this version of the Quest, Gilson provides an in-depth analysis of the specific spirituality of *The Quest of the Holy Grail* by comparing it with that of Saint Bernard of Clairvaux, the recognized inspiration for Cistercian mysticism. He finds in this very text that the holy Grail "is the grace of the Holy Ghost."

This is extremely important. In another study Gilson says, "It's an alteration of the meaning of the entire work to interpret a symbol of Grace

---

*Étienne Gilson, "The Mysticism of Grace," *Romania*, vol. 51 [Paris], 321 ff.

(the Grail) as if it were a question of a symbol of God."* Because the Grail is not God, it is not even a likeness, and it is consequently of no importance to know whether or not the sacred vessel held the blood of Christ. Therefore the knights who started quests with the goal of discovering the Grail-object followed a false trail and were unsuccessful. Furthermore, throughout the length of the story in developments that appear incoherent or even contradictory, knights engage in seeking a treasure, that mysterious as it may be, never conceals itself from the eyes of its seekers. The Grail shows itself constantly, whether for the purpose of guiding the searcher, or for healing, comforting, or feeding. What's more, none of the characters are ignorant of the location of the Grail, the castle of Corbénic, and the majority of knights go there, which is not to say that they succeeded in learning anything. Galahad himself, the hero of the Cistercian Quest, was born at Corbénic and raised there. He would have had no problem finding his way back to Corbénic after journeying to King Arthur's court for his initiation to the Round Table.

Furthermore, this provides the explanation for how those in the presence of the Grail react to it in accordance with their individual temperaments and states of grace. Gawain is scolded both because of his predominantly sensual nature and his refusal to accept the sacraments of the Church, the source of grace. The knights who die piously during the course of their quests—often because they fight one another without recognizing with whom they are fighting—are sinners obscured by their faults, but who reconcile with God in their final moments; thus Yvain found his eternal salvation in his death. Certain individuals, who are sinners but repent, such as Perceval and Bohort, are placed out of any danger and attain a mystical state that, despite being imperfect, places them above the run-of-the-mill human being. In fact, the sole person not to seek the Grail, despite what he said himself, is Lancelot of the Lake. But we have seen that what Lancelot sought in reality was Guinivere, who embodied his personal vision of the Grail. He is thus outside of the game, hence the privileges granted him, in particular the honor of being Galahad's father.

*Étienne Gilson, *Les Idées et les Lettre* (Paris: Vrin, 1932).

By this reckoning the tale of *The Quest of the Holy Grail* by the pseudo–Walter Map, and only this tale, is a remarkable utilization of mythological and novelesque themes to express a Christian conception of the universe. According to Gilson this quest is in no way a search for knowledge, but a quest for pure and tender love, because in the entire Augustinian and Bernadian school, "cognitive formulas are only metaphors designating affective states." The high adventure in which the Arthurian heroes participate, symbolizing to various degrees human beings surrendered to the quotidian, is brought here to a purely affective spiritual experience, that culminates in ecstasy, the "supreme efflorescence of the life of grace within us."

This Grail is nothing but grace generously and lovingly given by God. It is up to human beings to seize this grace on the fly and make something of it. This is not the Augustinian conception of grace that is jealously reserved by God for those of his choosing, it is the Bernadian—and Cistercian—grace that supports free will. All the knights receive this grace, but some do not make use of it or do so only clumsily. So, as Étienne Gilson asserts, since the Grail is not at all an "earthly object" but a manifestation of divine love, what matters is not finding it—this is something within everyone's grasp—but of discovering it and making it one's foremost revelation.

Therefore, when wishing to understand this particular version of the Quest by the pseudo-Map, one must never lose sight of the fact that the Grail is purely a visual symbol. This fits in perfectly with the original outline of the Quest in which the object had very little importance and was considered as only one of the elements in the unfolding of the plot. It could almost be said that the Grail, in all its forms and as an object (in the strictest etymological sense of the word), is only a carrot that is placed before the donkey to make it move forward. The Cistercian Grail is of this nature, even if it is divine grace: it is an encouragement to going beyond oneself, an act of sublimation, this is the appeal of God. It is for each to answer according to his own temperament. *"The Quest of the Holy Grail,"* says Étienne Gilson again, "is the search for the secrets of God that are unknown without grace."

That said, *The Quest of the Holy Grail* by the pseudo-Map picks up the adventures sketched out in the preceding versions and is content with letting them serve as the elucidation of this new conception of spirituality. Everything begins, or continues rather, at Arthur's court, Camelot, on the day of Pentecost. Custom had it that the traditional feast could only begin after a miraculous adventure had occurred.

Now, on the Perilous Seat, this phrase appears: "Four hundred fifty-four years after the passion of Jesus Christ this seat will find its master on the day of Pentecost." Furthermore it will be noted that this dating, which can be considered as fantastic, or symbolic, has the merit of resituating the adventure in its historic context, in the era of the real historical Arthur, that is to say, around the year 500 in southwest Great Britain. It seems that the author of the *Quest* was perfectly familiar with the origin of the Arthurian tradition.

It is then that a squire announces that a floating block of red marble has just appeared on the river, in which is thrust a marvelous sword. A phrase written on the stone states that the sword may only be drawn from the stone by he who is the best knight in the world. It is obvious that the floating stone is a theme borrowed from a Celtic story. There are numerous lives of Breton Saints in which one witnesses the arrival of an evangelist on a stone trough or a floating stone. As for the sword thrust in the stone, this is a double of the trial imposed on Arthur during his enthronement. It is therefore a ritual of sovereignty, with the difference being that this concerns a royalty of the spiritual kind rather than temporal as was the case for Arthur.

As the best knight in the world is Lancelot, according to all those in attendance, he is asked to pull out the sword. But Lancelot refuses. Arthur then asks Gawain to attempt the test. Gawain obeys his uncle, but unwillingly and, of course, he fails. At this moment a gentleman arrives bringing with him an adolescent youth who is none other than Galahad. The doors and windows of the festhall close immediately but an astounding light remains inside the room. Galahad seats himself without any ill effect on Seat Perilous, then the Holy Grail appears, hidden beneath a veil, and procures for the guests the best possible food and drink. After the festival the young Galahad easily withdraws the sword from the marvelous stone and all recognize him as Lancelot's son, whereupon Guinivere simultaneously experiences great feelings of pride and jealousy.

Lancelot's position in this episode is worse than ambiguous. He knows full well that he is not the hero of the Quest, which doesn't prevent him from attempting the adventure in an almost desperate fashion. But he effaces himself before his son whom he knighted but a short time earlier. Gawain also appears to have understood that he will not amount to anything. The royal way opens before Galahad, the predestined one, the pure one, before whom all spells are broken. He will therefore be the one who shows the way. The others will try to follow him.

Because all the knights decide to depart on the Quest, King Arthur, saddened, witnesses the departure of his companions. He knows full well that not all will return. And the queen makes her tender good-byes to Lancelot. The atmosphere of the court is of an imminent ending. Henceforth, nothing will be as it was in Arthur's kingdom.

For in the mind of the author of the *Quest*, as well as in the mind of the author of the last branch of the cycle, the *Mort d'Arthur*, the departure of Arthur's knights on this impossible mission constitutes the ineluctable end of their earthly adventures. Lancelot, the best terrestrial knight, must make way for Galahad, the celestial knight. The Arthurian universe, admirably symbolized by the Round Table, is only one step toward an ideal society that will no longer be of this world. As a projection of the Last Supper, then the Round Table, another feast awaits the elect, that of the Unreal Palace in which the guests share divine light, ecstasy, and the full and complete "communion" of heaven and Earth.

The author concerns himself first of all with Galahad. The young man receives the magic shield that will aid him in achieving his destiny. Then he reaches the Castle of the Maidens: there seven knights hold as prisoners the "maidens" that they kidnap or who stray into their neighborhood—forcing them to commit fornication. Galahad engages the seven knights in combat and is victorious. The fleeing seven knights are then killed by Gawain. But Galahad regrets their fate because "they could have made amends." In any case the "maidens" have been freed.

What we are dealing with here is the deliberate intention to Christianize a pagan myth. The "Castle of the Maidens" is the equivalent of the "Land of Fairy" or the Isle of Avalon, that paradisical island described so often in tales that are Celtic or of Celtic origin, an isle that has escaped the grip of time, where marvelous and sensually alluring women lull travelers with the shady delights of an ambiguous Eden. But all at once, in the Cistercian perspective, the fairies become diabolical embodiments. It is true that from the thirteenth century on the prisons and pyres of the Inquisition safeguarded orthodox Christianity against any nostalgia for earlier pagan beliefs. The "maidens," in the medieval sense of the word "unmarried women," are no longer fairies, beings endowed with supernatural powers, but innocent victims of male lust. The Land of Fairy of the ancient myths has been turned into a simple brothel where subjugated women do the will of men, who are themselves regarded as devils. Now Galahad, by his very nature, exorcises demons. It is inevitable that he will drive the demons from this castle. But he is content with driving them off: he doesn't seek the death of the sinner, hence his regret for the treatment inflicted upon them by Gawain. In fact, Galahad's quest is never bloody. Galahad, though he possesses the necessary strength, is never a warrior. He is only the purifier. This is the great innovation of the Cistercian Quest with respect to the previous versions, *Perlesvaus* in particular, which were animated by the spirit of the Crusades. We are in full contemplative mysticism here. But since in the ancient Quest the military aspect was inextricably intertwined with the sexual aspect, this latter aspect is also dropped. In short, Galahad, by delivering the "maidens" closes the brothels and establishes in their place convents of nuns. And these maidens, instead of contributing to the "warrior's rest," that is to say, the perpetuation of the warrior spirit by means of recreation (or re-creation), participate in the pacification of the universe, thus preparing for the coming of the Kingdom of God. The great innovation is that the mechanism unloosed by Galahad is the recuperation of sexual and warrior energies for Christian ends through repentance and the sublimation of desires.

Meanwhile Lancelot continues his solitary quest. Despite his good-will, he cannot tolerate the presence of the Grail. He witnesses an aston-ishing scene in a chapel in which a wounded, sick knight is healed by the appearance of the holy vessel. But Lancelot falls into a cataleptic state and lies stretched out upon the floor unable to move. He feels cursed and goes to confess to a hermit, promising to amend his ways.

Perceval, whose youth is not recounted here, also finds himself involved in adventures. A recluse, who reveals herself to be his aunt, explains certain things concerning the Holy Grail to him and implores him to preserve his virginity, for lack of which he would come to resem-ble Lancelot who, "through fevers of the flesh and lust has long since lost any hope of attaining what all the others strive for today." He is witness to a ceremony in a chapel during which he sees King Mordrain, the "maimed king." Then he faces various ruses of the Devil who seeks to drown him. Finally, a young girl invites him onto her boat and intoxi-cates him. He is about to succumb to temptation when, seeing his sword's pommel, makes the sign of the cross: everything disappears. He sees that the young girl was one of the devil's aspects. Then, in mortifi-cation, he carves a wound on his thigh, which is a symbolic gesture sig-nifying that he castrated himself, at least psychically.

The tale returns to Lancelot who strives vainly to learn the truth, and also to Gawain who courageously continues pursuing his quest with no hope of success. Then Bohort, Lancelot's cousin and repentant sinner, endowed with a ferocious will, takes his turn at center stage. Bohort emerges victorious from numerous adventures that constitute many ini-tiatory trials, struggles against the ruses of the Devil, and manages to escape a great temptation. Bohort, undoubtedly the most human of the three ultimate victors of the Quest, represents both the strength and the weakness of the Christian confronted by both the imperatives of evan-gelical law and the needs of the body. Ceaselessly vacillating between body and spirit, ceaselessly tormented by conflicting desires, Bohort nevertheless courageously continues to advance and never loses sight of his ultimate goal, which is, in this context, contemplation of the Grail.

Following numerous adventures, during which many of Arthur's knights meet their deaths, Galahad, Perceval, and Bohort discover the marvelous Ship of Solomon and the Sword of the Strange Belt, and learn the history of the Tree of Life whose wood was used in the construction of the ship. They see a white stag who is no longer a pagan god, the remote image of the religion of the cervidae hunters, but the personification of Jesus Christ, surrounded by four lions who are the four apostles. They are forced to battle hardily against their enemies, and they also learn that a sick young girl can only be cured by the blood of a young virgin who can only be the sister of Perceval. This latter, once found, agrees to the sacrifice. She gives her blood to the invalid and dies a short while later. This is an element that remains from the original version of the Quest; healing is dependent upon the blood of a new victim, but the idea of ritual vengeance has disappeared. Finally, the three companions go their separate ways.

During this time Lancelot has been pursuing his deceptive route. He meets his son Galahad and sails with him for several days. But Galahad goes off toward his destiny and Lancelot is alone again, leading the life of a wanderer. He reaches the Castle of the Grail where a voice bids him enter for he will find a portion of what he has long desired to see. He combats a host of illusory lions and finds himself in the center of the castle, but everything looks empty and abandoned. Then through a half-open door he hears music and the words of a strange ritual, and he sees an amazing light. He tries to push the door open and enter. The door doesn't budge. And the voice tells him: "Flee Lancelot, do not enter, you mustn't attempt to do so. And if you break this prohibition you will regret it" (Béguin, trans., 224). It is obvious that a ritual is taking place in the room to which Lancelot is forbidden access. Through this experience he gains the understanding that his vision of the Grail will always be imperfect. He has been allowed as far as the doorway, he has even seen the marvelous light emanating from inside, but that is all he is permitted. In the author's mind, Lancelot certainly benefited from grace, but in a form that a Pascalian Jansenist would have said was a sufficient grace that was not effective. For despite his intent, that is to say, his free will, Lancelot is expressly excluded from the mysteries of the Grail. He doesn't obtain the effective grace that would allow him to understand, or rather experience the supreme ecstasy of mystical union with God. And the text is clear enough on this subject: Lancelot bears the fault of having enjoyed a shameful relationship with Queen Guinivere. He has mended his ways, certainly, he has promised to renounce his sin—a promise he doesn't keep, by the way—he has received absolution, but this is not enough. Exiled from the benefits of grace as represented by the Grail is he who has chosen something else. Now, it is well known that at the bottom of his heart Lancelot has always made Guinivere his first choice. In *The Quest of the Holy Grail* we find ourselves in strict opposition to the mystical eroticism of the troubadours whereby one attains divine love through the experience of human love. In the Cistercian vision of the Grail there is no place for profane love. One must ascend immediately to the higher state. Hence Lancelot's partial defeat. He is not rejected nor punished. But he has reached the end of his possibilities. He then realizes that his quest is over and returns to Arthur's court. It is there that later, in the tale of *La Mort d'Arthur* that is the logical sequel to the *Quest*, that he falls back into his sinful relationship with Guinivere. But could he do otherwise?

The adventure will be terminated by Galahad, Bohort, and Perceval who are finally reunited and who will succeed to three different degrees at the test of the broken sword. Galahad heals the wounded king and the three companions are admitted to the secret liturgy of the Grail in the Castle of Corbénic. The kingdom recovers its prosperity because the spell, that is to say, the curse, that weighed it down has been lifted. But there is a second initiatory voyage to be made. Galahad, Perceval, and Bohort embark on Solomon's ship and make landfall at the marvelous palace of Sarras. It is here that Galahad is crowned king of the Grail, thus achieving what he had begun by sitting in the Perilous Seat of the Round Table at Camelot. It is also here that Galahad is given permission to contemplate what is inside the Grail. "As soon as he cast his eyes upon it he started to tremble, for his mortal flesh perceived spiritual things." And since that vision is more than a man can bear, Galahad, after embracing Perceval and asking Bohort to give his regards to his father

Lancelot, falls to his knees and dies. "The moment Galahad died a great marvel occurred: his two companions distinctly saw a hand that came down from heaven, without seeing the body to which it was attached. It went directly to the holy vessel, took it, and the Lance, and carried them off to heaven, so that since then no man can be so bold as to claim to have seen the Holy Grail" (Béguin trans., 251).

Once Galahad is buried Perceval goes to a hermitage located not far from the city of Sarras and takes religious orders. Bohort follows him there but doesn't become a monk. At the end of a year and three days Perceval dies. Bohort has him buried next to his sister and Galahad, then, as sole witness to the marvels of the Grail, he returns to Arthur's court. He will play a preeminent role, in the company of his cousin Lancelot, in the final Arthurian adventures. As for King Arthur, he has the events related by Bohort set down in writing.

This ending of *The Quest of the Holy Grail* is obviously completely symbolic. The outline of the original Quest is recognizable since Galahad heals the wounded king: thus the vengeance—or the redemption—is accomplished by the chosen one, he who was awaited. Henceforth the kingdom will recover its prosperity. But this is a profane redemption, sociological and magical as opposed to religious. The author of the *Quest* is the only one, among all the writers who utilized the Grail theme, to have proposed a second conclusion, one that takes place in the mysterious city of Sarras. And Galahad, the true leader of the undertaking, is the only one to be given permission to contemplate the interior of the holy vessel. He dies because of it, but is entirely beatified, having been, from this gesture, conveyed from the human state to one that is quasi divine. He can no longer tolerate earthly life for he has seen "celestial things." He has passed to the *other side.*

However, there is nothing tragic about this death, or rather, passage. To the contrary, it is triumphant and freely accepted by Galahad. His mission is ended, and as he was only there to provide the example, he no longer has any reason to live. The author takes advantage of the situation to cause the definitive disappearance of the Grail. Regarding this "ascension" of the Grail and the Lance an astonishing parallel can be noted: at the end of the Arthurian epic, Arthur's sword, the symbol of sovereignty, that had been entrusted to the king by the Lady of the Lake, a water deity in other words, is taken back by a hand that emerges from the water to carry it off. Temporal power comes from below, from the depths of the water, and returns there. Spiritual power, or grace if one prefers, comes from on high, from the heights of heaven, and returns there. The Grail Quest is integrated perfectly into the Arthurian tale, even if it is recuperated by Cistercian ideology, even if it serves to demonstrate that the spiritual search has nothing in common with the will to power.

Perceval's death later on can also be explained by the hero's state of grace. Hierarchically he is second in the Quest, the closest to Galahad. In this version he is truly and unquestionably a virgin. He therefore shares Galahad's saintliness. There is a slight difference though. Galahad dies while in mystical trance while Perceval dies in meditation and prayer. He is closer to humanity than Galahad. As the *Quest's* author was distrustful of the character, he did not want to make Perceval the first to cross the finish line in the race to the Grail. However, to a certain extent he serves humanity as a model. Indeed, the author seems to be offering an alternate path whereby saintliness can be attained by means other than the ecstatic sacrifice of Galahad, which assumes an absolute mystical union. It is enough to respect the laws of the Church, keeper of the evangelical message, but to do that it is necessary to become a monk. Perceval's path is a fine example of monastic propaganda within the reach of everyone.

Bohort doesn't die. Even in the last branch of the Arthurian epic, he survives all the others. He is the privileged witness, thanks to whom we know the story. He is in the image of the simple man of faith, a sinner like everyone else, certainly not a virgin, stained with imperfections but honest, sincere, and loyal. He represents the third way possible for salvation, a way that is not negligible because it ensures the remembrance and permanence of spiritual success. The Grail has perhaps disappeared, Galahad and Perceval are dead, but Bohort is there to tirelessly repeat the message he bears. Symbolically it is Bohort from whom the line of Grail seekers issues, who, even in our time, are implored—more or less consciously—to resume their quest.

The Quest of the Holy Grail by the pseudo-Map is a unique work. There has been no imitation or adaptation. In itself it constitutes the end of a cycle, and one cannot go back there, at least in terms of the spiritual context of its time. It is a Christian, essentially monastic work. Some claim that the tale has underlying elements borrowed from Catharism, but a painstaking search has revealed none. Nothing is more orthodox and more in conformance to thirteenth-century spirituality than this version of the Quest. The elements that appear bizarre, of which there are a few, have been borrowed from the original outline when the author obviously couldn't ignore or neglect them, since he built his work on earlier fictional data. But these elements, far from presenting similarities to Cathar doctrine (about which not much is known), seem, in contrast, far removed from this doctrine. If there is any trace of Manichaeanism it is the classic separation between Good and Evil, a perfectly orthodox separation in the doctrine of the Roman Catholic Church.

As for saying that the Grail of the *Quest* of the pseudo-Map is the true Grail, that which has attained its highest degree of perfection, that's something else entirely. Also, can there be a true Grail?

FOUR

THE GERMANO-IRANIAN GRAIL: WOLFRAM VON ESCHENBACH'S *PARZIVAL*

Wolfram von Eschenbach, a German poet who was most likely of Bavarian origin, lived around the beginning of the thirteenth century and served under the landgrave Hermann of Thuringia, who died around the year 1217. He was the author of several unfinished works and one complete poem, *Parzival*, composed between 1197 and 1210, in which he undertook the tale of the quest of the hero brought to light by Chrétien de Troyes. But if it is obvious that he was adapting Chrétien, even translating him literally in certain spots, it is beyond question that Chrétien's *Perceval* was not his sole source. And it is true that the problem concerning Wolfram's influences has received no definitive solution.

In fact, the entire beginning of his work, concerning Parzival's father, has no points in common with Chrétien or his successors. That Wolfram himself may have invented the character in an effort to provide a preface to his hero's adventures is possible, but other elements, namely the intervention of a brother (or half brother rather) of Parzival, a half-breed of European and Muslim (Iraqi) descent, or even the mention of Loherangrin, son of Parzival, appear to have been borrowed from sources completely foreign to Chrétien as well as to the original Celtic archetype. However, not only does the Celtic outline remain intact, but Wolfram added details that are clearly of Celtic origin, such as the specific idea of blood vengeance that is not found in Chrétien's work, that perhaps Chrétien was aware of but deemed wise not to retain.

What is certain is that the influence of Robert de Boron and Glastonbury Abbey on Wolfram's work is null. However, and this is not the least of problems, this work bears the indirect mark of the Plantagenets. In fact, Wolfram takes pains throughout his tale to flatter the powerful house of Anjou, the known cradle of the Plantagenet dynasty, and he makes Parzival's mother Herzeloyde a titulary queen of three states, Norgals, Waleis, and Anjou. This is fairly significant. And as Wolfram himself was quite far from the Plantagenet circle of influence, it must be assumed that the Angevin references come from a source other than Chrétien de Troyes, for the latter, although indirectly enfeoffed to the English dynasty, makes no specific mention of it. By his own acknowledgment Wolfram was inspired by a model that he moreover opposes to Chrétien de Troyes: "Master Chrétien de Troyes has told this story but altered it in so doing, and Kyot, who transmitted the true story to us, was irked by this for good reason."* Throughout his work Wolfram cites this Kyot the Provencal who "wrote in French." This detail can appear surprising; the people of Provence at that time generally wrote in Occitan. Critics, basing their arguments on the fact that Wolfram was speaking of Provins en Brie and on the very name Kyot, which is the Germanic variant of the French Guiot or Guillot, have attempted to identify this mysterious Provencal with a known poet, Guiot of Provins, author of a satiric Bible that lacks for neither verve nor ferocity. This appears quite dubious. It is necessary to confess that we know nothing of this Kyot the Provencal who is mentioned nowhere else.

It is not out of the question that Kyot may have been a ruse created by Wolfram. Numerous authors of this era claimed authenticity for the

---

*Ernest Tonnelat, trans., *Parzival* (Paris: Aubier Montaigne, 1934), vol. 2, 342.

stories they told alleging their provenance from an earlier author whose name they cited. And when it wasn't true they invented this name, or else usurped that of a known individual (such as the attribution of *The Quest of the Holy Grail* to a Walter Map who lived thirty years earlier). Now in the case of Kyot-Guiot the name could perhaps be a ruse. Indeed the names Guiot and Guillot are connected to the root *guille* (the Anglo-Saxon *vile*, the English *wile*), an old French word that has disappeared from the modern language that means both an idea of deception and of silliness. And there are numerous examples in twelfth- and thirteenth-century literature of word games using the word *guille* and the names of Guillaume and its diminutives such as Guiot and Guillot. One could also cite the famous proverb "Tel croit guiller Guillot que Guillot guille" (Littré).*

Why not accept the fact that Wolfram, having found a different version of the Quest somewhere, made use of it by inventing an imaginary personage?

Nevertheless it is difficult to cast doubt on the reality of a contribution from a source other than Chrétien de Troyes in the elaboration of *Parzival.* Wolfram is somewhat mum concerning this source: "The illustrious master Kyot found among some abandoned manuscripts in Toledo, the substance of this story, copied in Arabic script. He had to learn the characters' A B C beforehand (the elements of magic writing according to Wolfram), but he never had recourse to necromancy. It was a great advantage that he had been baptized—otherwise this tale would have remained unknown. There is not in fact a pagan wise enough to reveal the nature of the Grail and tell us how one came to know its secret virtues" (Tonnelat trans., vol. 2, 23).

Basically, for Wolfram the original outline of the Quest and especially the great secrets of the Grail have a precise origin: they come from the East by the intermediary of an Arabic manuscript. This is quite in contradiction with the source of *Perceval* by Chrétien de Troyes, which derives from an incontestable Celtic archetype. One could moreover

---

* He thinks to gull Guillot who Guillot gulls—translation.

believe that this Eastern attribution is a hoax by Wolfram, a concession to the fashions of the time in Germany that were already marked by a nebulous Easternism. But this is not at all the case: there are numerous landmark details in the tale of *Parzival* that prove to the contrary an indisputable Iranian influence on the Quest. This is why the Grail of Wolfram von Eschenbach, despite its Celtic structure, should be considered as a Germanic-Iranian Grail.

These details are numerous and disturbing. There is first of all the wounding of Anfortas, the Fisher King (whose name, incidentally derives from the Latin *Infirmitas*). Wolfram tells us the pain of the Fisher King's wound is intolerable when the weather is freezing. And when Parzival cures him, he clearly appears with the features of Indra, who, when the Aryans were in the northern lands before beginning their migration toward India, *was the god who made the ice melt*, a regenerative solar deity.

The Fisher King himself can be considered as the correspondent of an Indian character. The goldfish is the first embodied manifestation of Vishnu as a creator, a symbol that converges with the image of the early Christians' *Ichthus*, representation of Jesus, the man/god. In the speculations of Tibetan Buddhism the goldfish symbolizes the creatures immersed in the ocean of *samsara* (the infernal cycle of reincarnations) that must be led by the Fisherman into the light and the Great Liberation.

In Wolfram—and nowhere else—Parzival's father leaves to fight in the East and meets his death near Baghdad. But he had a son while there, the Feirefiz with whom Parzival will accomplish his mission to the Castle of the Grail. It is surely not by chance that the author places so much emphasis on the adventures of Parzival's father and the participation of his half-white, half-black brother whose Oriental nature is so obvious.

Wolfram places certain adventures of Gawain in the magic palace of Klingsor, an individual who later takes on an extraordinary importance in the opera by Richard Wagner. Now Klingsor's castle, meticulously described by Wolfram, has a surprising resemblance to descriptions of the Buddhist monasteries in Kabulistan, especially the palace of Kapisa, with its fantastically wheeled throne—similar to the Bed of the Marvelous—the gigantic stupa, and all the rest.* There is little likelihood that Wolfram von Eschenbach visited these faraway lands. The possibility that he invented these descriptions can be ruled out. Therefore he must have gotten them from someone else.

That isn't all. In Iran there is a story that is of completely Manichaean spirit, the *Story of the Pearl*, that deals with the quest and initiation of a poorly dressed and fatherless young man. It could be said that this story line appears in all folk traditions. Yes, but the Manichaean traces, the incessant struggle between God and the Enemy, Day and Night, is all very explicit in Wolfram's *Parzival* while is it almost completely absent in the other versions, even the Cistercian version. It would be rightfully said that Wolfram has systematically accentuated the Manichaean aspect of Parzival's quest. After all, when Hitler conceived the plan to stage Wagner's *Parzival*, his favorite opera, an opera directly descended from Wolfram, on the day of the final victory of Nazism over the Judeo-plutocratic dark forces, it was not without a valid reason.

Let's take this even further. In Wolfram's work the Castle of the Grail is named Munsalvæsche (Mount Salvation). He has given us a detailed description that begs to be compared to the description of Manichaean citadels, in particular that of the Ruh-I-Sal-Shwâdeha on Lake Hamun located on the border between Iran and Afghanistan.

Now, taking into account that Ruh-I means "mount," wouldn't Munsalvæsche be an exact correlation of Ruh-I-Sal-Shwâdeha? This similarity is much too exact to be due to chance.

One can understand why researchers—almost exclusively Germans—have patiently explored the Cathar citadel of Montségur, whose very name can be compared to Munsalvæsche. The mysterious mission of the larger-than-life figure Otto Rahn, probably encouraged and supported by high ranking Nazi officials, concerning Grail research at Montségur and the Cathar regions, was not invented by journalists

---

* Josef Strzygowski, *Asien's Minaturenmalerei* (Klagenfurt, Austria: 1933).

seeking the sensational. It certainly took place, even if Otto Rahn's life is somewhat obscure and easily lends itself to numerous interpretations.*

Much could be said about the assertions made by the hermit Trevrizent to Parzival during his visit. He told him in fact that the Grail was first guarded by "angels who were neither good nor evil." The hermit then declared that he had been lying and that the story about the angels wasn't true. This lie forms part of the initiatory game in which the neophyte must himself tell true from false, and real from imaginary, but it nonetheless remains true that this story of angels that are neither good nor evil has a Manichaean odor about it. There is no need for surprise at next seeing Munsalvæsche guarded by knights of the Grail who are none other than Templars.

Finally there is the Grail itself. In *Parzival,* and in this text alone, the Grail is a precious stone on which rests a dove identified as the Holy Ghost. The name of this stone, at least according to Wolfram's claim, is *lapsit exillis* in the text, which needs to be corrected as *lapis exillis.* One is now convinced that Wolfram, whose French while serviceable left something to be desired, committed numerous misinterpretations in his translation of Chrétien de Troyes's tale (the most well-known being the tray translated as "knives," when the object in question was a carving plate). Thus the following explanation has been proposed for the replacement of the vessel containing the blood of Christ, or Chrétien's simple container, by a precious stone: Wolfram would have taken the precious stones adorning the Grail for the Grail itself. This explanation doesn't hold up. The entire context of Wolfram's tale justifies the choice of a stone. There is first of all an alchemical allusion, *lapis exillis* being quite close to *lapis elixir,* which is the term used by the Arabs to designate the Philosopher's Stone. Next the stone of the Grail guarded by angels irresistibly summons thoughts of the Ka'aba stone in Mecca, and calls to mind other stories of this type. One is reminded in particular of

---

* Otto Rahn, *Kreuzzug gegen den Gral* (Fribourg: 1933). See the popularized but extremely well-documented work of Christian Bernadac, *Le Mystère Otto Rahn* (Paris: France-Empire, 1978).

the tradition that states that the Grail was carved into the form of a vessel from the gigantic emerald that fell from Lucifer's forehead at the time of his revolt against heaven and fall into the abyss. In addition, René Nelli, on this subject, has suggested lapis exillis could be seen as a deformation of *lapis e coelis*, that is to say, "stone fallen from the heavens." This hypothesis appears acceptable taking the context of the story into account, and it must be said that it has its attractions.

But, in addition, Wolfram's Grail/Stone bears a great resemblance to the Manichaean jewel, the Buddhist *padma mani*, the jewel found in the heart of the lotus that is the solar symbol of the Great Liberation and which can also be found in the Indian traditions concerning the Tree of Life. It is also the Chwarna of which the *Avesta* speaks, magical, divine, and multiform, "that causes the waters to gush from their springs, the plants from the earth, the wind to chase the clouds, men to be born, and guides the stars and the moon in their courses." Wolfram's Grail/Stone possesses the same qualities as the Chwarna. Moreover, on this stone rests a dove who has just placed the grain of Hanna there. It so happens that on the Grail/Stone the dove brings a sacramental host on Good Friday, which is, as if by chance, the resurrection day of the Nordic sun. And what can be said of the Buddhist paintings representing the Divine Virgin bearing the jewel that dispenses joy? In Wolfram's work the Grail bearer's name is Repanse de Schoye, in other words Reconsideration of Joy. All of these accumulated details constitute precise facts and not ingenious hypotheses. We must conclude that Wolfram von Eschenbach consciously and intentionally transformed Chrétien de Troyes's "receptacle" into the *Stone Fallen from heaven*. And did so from an incontestably Manichaean perspective.

This is the appropriate time to touch on the necessary question of the Cathars and their eventual connection to the Grail myth. Much nonsense has been written and spoken on this subject. In any case there can be no connection between Catharism and the Celtic Grail as it has appeared to us in the wake of the archetypal text. The Cathar's system of thought is Manichaean and their philosophy is dualist, beyond question. Now the Celtic system of thought is constructed on a stubborn refusal of Manichaeanism; their philosophy is a monism. The two are absolutely incompatible. Chrétien's *Perceval*, the Welsh *Peredur*, the Cluny Order's *Perlesvaus*, and the Cistercian versions have no relationship with Catharism and its specific conceptions.

But the question does not arise in the same fashion for Wolfram von Eschenbach's *Parzival*. It is the sole version of the Quest that bears the mark of Manichaeanism. It is the sole version of the Quest that can be compared—with the utmost caution—to the beliefs and conceptions of the Cathars. It was perhaps the mysterious Kyot the Provencal that led Wolfram to this metamorphosis of the initial theme. As an Occitain he should have been familiar with the Cathar world of Occitan; the door was opened toward the Manichaean and even toward the Buddhist East.

Of course we must discard at the outset the hypothesis that Montségur was the Castle of the Grail. First of all the Grail, as said before, is only a concept, a symbolic image that can assume all forms and which necessarily sits outside space and time. Next, by making precise reference to Wolfram's text, any so-called worship of the Grail at Montségur couldn't have taken place until after *Parzival* was written since the old citadel hadn't been restored by the Cathars until several years before the crusade raised against them by the ever-so-Christian king of northern France. The French king was bent on sweeping away these undesirables who intended to establish their society in the path of another society that was in the midst of a full-scale territorial expansion. It is not my intention to pass judgment upon the Cathars; others have assumed that burden, with a margin for error that is always cause for concern. I seek only to bring to light the points of agreement between the facts of Catharism and the facts of Wolfram's *Parzival*.

First of all, the Cathars and *Parzival* hold in common an obsession with purity. Even though Parzival is not a virgin—nor even chaste, by the way—he is nevertheless obsessed with the conquest of absolute purity. This is the reason Wolfram has him marry Blanchfleur's equivalent, Condwiramurs. The marriage makes their relationship wholesome from a moral point of view. Parzival's purity, which was only simple naiveté in Chrétien's Perceval, allows him to ascend through all the stages of initiation and become the incontestable king of the Grail. And his son Loherangrin, the knight of that very symbolic animal the swan, will continue this conquest that will force him to part from his wife, the duchess of Brabant, because she has broken the terrible taboo concerning his name and origins. When one is pure one has no need of a name. And purity leads to perfection, the supreme goal of Catharism. The Grail king has attained this stage; he has definitively resolved the dilemma of good and evil by denying evil. It is the victory of Ahura-Mazda over Ahriman, God over Satan, the light over the darkness. And what's to be said about the Grail bearer who is called, according to Wolfram, Repanse de Schoye? She is in no way comparable with Chrétien's young girl, with Elaine, the daughter of the Fisher King who conceives Galahad out of her embrace with Lancelot, with the disturbing dual-sexed empress who is revealed to be in reality Peredur's cousin. Repanse de Schoye is chaste. She is pure. She can die but will be reborn from her own ashes like the phoenix. She is nothing more than a visual image of purity or perfection, perhaps analogous to the image referred to by the troubadours of the ungraspable Cathar Church that they called their "Lady," or their "Azimant"—in other words their "aimant" [lover—translator's note]—with all the wordplay and esoteric extensions that that term can entail.

There is still the question that Parzival must ask to cure the Fisher King. He doesn't have to inquire, as in the other versions, about the mysteries of the Grail but must simply ask, "King, from what are you suffering?" In Wolfram's version the ideal of compassion is the key to salvation. This emphasis on compassion derives from a remote Buddhist tradition whereby souls can finally emerge from the jaws of the vice of carnal matter (Indo-Buddhist *samsara*) to ascend to the ecstatic joys of nonexistence in the Eternal Light of an unnamable and unreachable God. Here the ritual is no longer Christian. It is not even Celtic. It is Cathar, by virtue of which it reunites with Eastern thought. Given the assumption that the individual soul doesn't exist and that only the universal soul has a reality, there is no individual salvation. Salvation can only concern humanity in its entirety. Thus it is everyone's duty to display compassion to one another, in order to reunify what has been sundered, in order to reawaken the pieces of the universal soul *(atman)* and let them share in the light. To achieve this reunification it is necessary to abolish all individual suffering, for earthly suffering is a satanic snare, a trap of matter, and an illusion. When Parzival cures the Fisher King, the latter does not die, as in the other versions of the Quest. On the contrary, Anfortas is rejuvenated and devotes himself to the service of the Grail. He who had been wounded in his sexual organs because he has enjoyed too much pleasure from them, finds himself abruptly regenerated by Parzival the Pure and he transcends his libido to the wonder of others. And everyone knows that in wonder there is awakening.* The Cathar baptism is that received when one touches the light that emanates from the Grail, considered as grace by the Cistercians. But grace is useless for Wolfram, as it is, moreover, for the Celts. Anyone, on the condition that their eyes are open, can share in the divine light.

It is from this perspective that it is necessary to examine the main character of the Esclarmonde of the Pyrenees legend. There are probably two Esclarmondes sharing one name. Nevertheless she is a Lady in White, an extremely astonishing synthesis of the mythic fairy of ancient times and the Cathar abbess. One was burned at the stake. The other didn't die but was miraculously transported to the mountains of Asia. Perhaps she later returned under the name and shape of Mélusine. But this myth simply recasts the myth of Repanse de Schoye, or rather they are the same with no way of telling which came first. And why are there so many doves on the pottery in Pyrenees grottoes, if not because they correspond to the image of the dove coming to rest every Good Friday on the lapis exillis, the Grail/Stone guarded by the Knights Templar of Munsalvæsche?

For Wolfram mystical and ritual concerns give way to speculations of an alchemical nature that aim to disengage the divine essence that sleeps in the heart of matter. This is pure Catharism. Wolfram claimed that the

---

* The point is clearer in the French as the word for awakening, *éveil,* is contained in the French word for wonder, *émerveillement*—translator's note.

manuscript found in Toledo by Kyot the Provencal had been written by a certain Flegetanis. This Flegetanis was of the line of Solomon. He was a Jew and most curious of all he wrote in Arabic. But we are told he was born of an Arab father. According to Jewish custom he was therefore Jewish through his mother. Wolfram was somewhat hard on Flegetanis:* "He worshiped a calf in which he saw a god." But, "he knew how to predict the disappearance of each star and the moment of its return" (Tonnelat trans., vol. 2, 24), which has led him to be classified as an astrologer by the commentators when it actually means that he had been initiated into a religion preaching reincarnation—such as Indian Buddhism—and the infernal cycle of *samsara*.

Most importantly, "there was, he said, an object called the Grail. He had clearly read its names in the stars. A band of angels had placed it upon the earth then soared off far above the stars. These angels were too pure to remain here below" (Tonnelat trans., vol. 2, 24). Reading such an assertion who couldn't doubt that the Grail of Wolfram von Eschenbach, supposedly revised and corrected through Flegetanis and Kyot the Provencal, wasn't comparable to the *consolamentum* of the Cathars? But let me repeat that this is the sole occasion in which an important point of concordance can be found between the Grail Quest and the Cathar experience.

In any case it seems that Wolfram thought the Grail myth to be clearly of pagan origin. If it is necessary to be a Christian to understand and explain it, its message nonetheless is delivered from the depths of the ages, a kind of *revelation* parallel to the revelations of the great religions, and a revelation with an undoubtably secret and marginal nature. This is what explains the unorthodox tone of Wolfram's work. The angels who, according to Flegetanis, brought the stone of the Grail are more than suspect. It is true that Flegetanis was incapable of understanding

* Flegetanis is a clumsy transcription of Falak-Thani, an Arabic expression meaning the second heaven, that of Mercury-Hermes, placed under the protection of the "messenger of the gods with S. Aïssa, that is to say, Jesus. This second heaven governs life and spiritual knowledge." Albert Ollivier, *Les Templiers* (Paris: le Seuil, 1958), 72.

since the tale he transcribed dated from "a very ancient time in which men were not yet protected by baptism against the fires of hell" (Tonnelat trans., vol. 2, 24). However, based on Wolfram's statements, Kyot the Provencal, reflecting on the angels departure concluded that the Grail had been entrusted to men "turned Christian by baptism and as pure as angels." It is then that

> Kyot, the master sage, sought in Latin books the place in which a people pure enough and with a strong enough tendency to a life of renunciation to become the guardians of the Grail could have lived. He read the chronicles of the kingdoms of Britain, France, and Ireland, and many others besides, until he found in Anjou that which he had been seeking. (Tonnelat trans., vol. 2, 25)

In this way Kyot, or Wolfram, attached a Judeo-Eastern myth to a Western, Celtic, and Anjou tradition, in other words the Arthurian universe that the Plantagenets contributed such a great deal to developing and spreading. In sum, Wolfram's tale follows an itinerary parallel to that of Robert de Boron's, but if this latter brought about the fusion of a pagan Celtic legend with the Christian legend of Joseph of Arimathea, Wolfram brought about the fusion of the pagan, Celtic legend with a Judeo-Eastern legend in which Christianity is singularly absent. That is because the Grail of Wolfram, even if a dove alights on it every Good Friday, no longer has anything in common with the ciborium and chalice of the Christian ritual of the Mass. With this explained the particular fate of this version of the Quest is no longer surprising. Its heretical connotations, and its bizarre extensions toward an Aryan mysticism, introduce the Templar guardians of the Grail as the fierce upholders of a racial purity. Thus Wolfram removes from the outset—and coldly eliminates—the heterogeneous elements who are forbidden access to the mysteries of the Grail.

In fact, Wolfram's *Parzival* is the most pagan of all the versions of the Quest, much more so than *Peredur* if one takes into account the fact that there have always been points of agreement between Celtic beliefs inherent to druidism and Christian beliefs such as they appeared in Ireland, Britain, and Brittany. With *Parzival* we are elsewhere. We are no longer in the West; we are in the Aryan and Manichaean East.

At the start of his novel Wolfram provides an abundant retelling of the adventures of Parzival's father, a certain Gahmuret, whose heroic figure irresistibly recalls that of Richard the Lion Hearted. Gahmuret travels to the East where he takes service with King Baruc of Baghdad. He leads a restless life and marries a native woman who gives him a son, Feirefiz. He returns to the West—Anjou of course—and meets individuals as diverse as Uther Pendragon, Arthur's father, the still adolescent Gawain, and other heroes of the Arthurian cycle, and even Morholt of Ireland mentioned in the story of Tristan. He marries Queen Herzeloyde, then departs anew for the East leaving his pregnant wife behind. He meets his death in a battle while Herzeloyde, mad with grief, gives birth to a son that she names Parzival.

This prologue that creates such a connection between the hero's paternal family and the East is found only in Wolfram's work. What is certain is that the author seems bent on explicitly displaying Gahmuret's ties with the house of Anjou and the characters of the Arthurian cycle. What is not known, however, is whether the theme of this prologue comes from elsewhere or whether the German poet invented it himself.

The sequel unfolds almost exactly as in Chrétien de Troyes's book. Herzeloyde, the "Old Lady," raises her son sheltered from the world and isolated from anything that would tempt him to take up arms. Of course the young Parzival encounters three knights who, in this version alone, are in pursuit of Meleagant who is guilty of kidnapping a woman. After his initial astonishment, the young man makes the knights explain the reasons for their arms and armor and thenceforth ceaselessly hounds his mother for permission to be knighted by King Arthur. Herzeloyde bestows upon him the famous pieces of advice, then she lets him leave after she has made certain to have him dress as a jester, who no one will take seriously. This detail appears only in this version of the Quest. Most importantly his mother tells him: "You should also know my son, that the audacious and magnificent Lähelin has taken possession of two of your hereditary lands, Waleis and Norgals, despite your princes. He has killed your prince Turkentals with his own hand. He has beaten your men or imprisoned them." Parzival swears to strike his enemy with his javelin. He then leaves without looking back and Herzeloyde dies of grief.

Herzeloyde's counsel takes on a completely different value here. Before her son leaves she alerts him to an act of vengeance he cannot leave unfulfilled. There is not a trace of this warning in Chrétien's book, nor in that of the Welsh author, in which the theme of revenge nevertheless predominates. Furthermore this Lähelin is somewhat mysterious. Should a derivative of the German word hell be seen in this name, a word meaning both the infernal region and the goddess of the lower realms? In this case Parzival's mission, accepted by his mother in exchange for her life, would be a veritable descent into hell, a kind of shamanistic voyage into the Otherworld to find a murderer and punish him. This theme is seen again in the Irish tale *The Voyage of Maelduin*, in which the hero reaches the famous Land of Fairy because he undertook his voyage with the objective of avenging his father's murder (Markale, *L'Épopée celtique d'Irlande*, 196–202).

So Parzival is on his way. He has the same adventures as Chrétien's Perceval. In Arthur's court his attire provokes a good number of gibes, which doesn't prevent him from killing the offensive knight, named here Ithier of Gaheviez. He is next welcomed by the aged lord Gurnemanz of Graharz (Gornemant de Goort) who teaches him how to use his weapons and ride a horse. An anecdote not found in *Perceval* shows us Parzival quite attracted to the beauty of Gurnemanz's daughter Liase. His host would be more than happy, moreover, to give his consent to their wedding. But Parzival resumes his journey, though still tormented by his desire for Liase, a desire that only grows stronger. He then makes his way to the castle of the beautiful Condwiramurs (Blanchefleur) with whom he immediately falls in love, but in a singular fashion. He starts by believing that Condwiramurs is Liase, after which he psychologically transfers his affections for Liase to Condwiramurs. Parzival fights the enemies of the young princess and delivers her from all danger. He resists all carnal temptations for Condwiramurs for two nights but on the third he succumbs. This is, of course, a kind of test that is very wide-spread in folktales.

Parzival could easily remain by Condwiramurs's side and forget the rest of his mission. But because he wishes to see his mother again he takes his leave. It is on account of this that he encounters the Fisher King, with a "hat of peacock feathers and lined with them inside" who invites him to spend the night. His entrance into the castle is accompanied by grotesque occurences and the atmosphere is quite strange here: "Amusement had been absent here since long date; the hearts of its inhabitants were given over to grief." These details concerning the sorrow of the inhabitants are not found in Chrétien's *Perceval* but conform perfectly to the tale of *Peredur* and the *Romance of Jauffré*.

Parzival is richly received by his host, the frail and wounded Fisher King. Wolfram provides a detailed account of everything that can be seen inside the castle, followed by a generous recounting of the Grail procession:

A page suddenly crossed the threshold bearing—a deeply moving spectacle—a lance from whose steel blood issued and ran down the shaft to his hand and disappeared into his sleeve. At this sight sobs and wails filled the citadel. The page, holding his lugubrious burden, made the circuit of the four walls and just as suddenly vanished through the door by which he had entered. At the far end of the room a steel door was thrown open through which a pair of noble maidens emerged. They were two blond virgins each bearing a golden candelabra in which a candle was burning. After them came a duchess and her companion carrying two ivory pedestals immediately followed by eight other ladies whose role was as follows: four carried large candles while the others effortlessly upheld a precious stone through which the sun traveled and which earned its name because of its luster. Two other princesses presented themselves in their turn, deliciously adorned. In their hands they carried two carving knives of an extraordinary white silver. After these came the princess. Her face shed such a glow that all believed it was sunrise. Upon an emerald green cushion she bore the root and blossoming of all one wished in paradise: the Grail transcending all earthly ideals. Repanse de Schoye was the name of the maiden worthy of carrying the Grail."*

This is no longer the meager procession described by Chrétien, involving a Grail that glows with a supernatural light whose enigmatic nature is only emphasized by the brevity of the description. We are equally far from the dryness of the Welsh author who emphasizes the dramatic nature of the scene. Wolfram isn't stingy with details, is mistaken concerning the Tray that is transformed here into two knives, and doesn't hesitate to name the Grail as a proper noun. There is perhaps no mystery remaining regarding the procession, except that the Grail itself, though mentioned twice and defined as the root and blossoming of all one wished in paradise, is still, to say the least, mysterious. Wolfram doesn't even say what shape it took on for this appearance. One learns afterward that the Grail furnishes the guests with food and drink. What is important in this sumptuous description is the accentuation of the solar character—already visible in Chrétien's work—of not only the Grail but the young woman carrying it.

And Parzival asks no questions. This does not prevent him from being led, with much deference, to a magnificent bed in which he spends a night tortured by an internal anguish that grips him for reasons unknown. The next morning the castle is deserted. He leaves, finds his horse already saddled, and takes his departure while an invisible page shouts after him: "May the hatred of the sun fall upon you, you silly goose. Why didn't you open your beak and question your host? You would have earned great glory." These invectives, not seen in Chrétien de Troyes's version, again emphasize the "sun." It would seem that for Wolfram the Grail procession was clearly a solar ritual of Buddhist-Manichaean appearence. If the Fisher King represents the setting sun casting its final rays, Parzival could be considered to be the young sun

* Maurice Wilmotte, trans. *Parzival* (Paris: 1933), 82–85.

about to rise and infuse new strength into the light. But by not asking questions, Parzival doesn't awaken and remains in the dark of night. The opportunity has been missed. This furnishes the explanation for a curse called down upon him: "May the hatred of the sun fall upon you." In any event, it has to be admitted that the context is hardly Christian. This particular example of the Grail paradise more resembles the heavenly orchard of ancient Iran, or even the Buddhist nirvana in which wishing is no longer possible as all desire has been abolished.

Perceval has no choice but to leave with the sword his host has entrusted to him as a very precious object. He meets a young woman weeping over the body of her dead lover. She is his cousin, here named Sigune. She reveals to him that the Fisher King's name is Anfortas and that his grandfather Titurel is still living. She also tells Parzival that if he had asked *the* question he would have healed the wounded king and earned great honor. She warns him that his sword, the one bestowed upon him by the Fisher King, will break and only the smith Trebuchet, who lives near the Lake spring, not far from Karnant (Kaer-Nant is a Welsh name that could well be Nantes, in any event it means "City of the Valley") will be able to make it whole again. Last, she gives Parzival the name of the Grail Castle: Munsalvæsche.

After leaving his cousin Parzival reconciles the young maiden from whom he had stolen the pie and a kiss with her friend Orsilus. Near Arthur's court he falls into an ecstatic trance upon seeing blood on the snow that reminds him of Condwiramurs (the anecdote is identical in Chrétien de Troyes's *Perceval*), knocks to the ground the knights sent to invite him to the court, and finally lets himself be led there by Gawan (the German Gawain). One detail that is lacking in Chrétien's account and curiously found here is that Ginover pardons Parzival for the slaying of Ithier of Gaheviez, the thief of the cup and the young hero's first victim. "While she spoke these words of pardon her eyes grew moist with tears, to this extent Ithier's death had brought pain to women" (Wilmotte trans., 123). Wolfram seems to have forgotten that by stealing the cup and spilling its contents over Ginover, Ithier had committed a serious outrage against the queen and called her sovereignty into question. But he obviously understood nothing of Ginover's sovereign duties.

While at Arthur's court Parzival completely forgets his mission. It is at this point that the "hideous Maiden on the Mule," here named Cundrie the Sorceress, comes on the scene. Her physical description equals that painted by Chrétien:

> Her nose was like a dog's. Two boars tusks jutted from her mouth that were a span each in length, and the bristly tufts of her eyebrows extended over her hairline. Cundrie had ears like a bear and her forbidding countenance hardly invited a lover's caress. This dainty darling had the paws of an ape with fingernails that were none too transparent. If I understand my author correctly they were hooked like the claws of a lion. (Wilmotte trans., 125)

There are two apparently important details in Wolfram's version that are missing from Chrétien's romance. First of all Cundrie is wearing a hat "made of peacock feathers" reminiscent of the Fisher King's. As is known peacock feathers are symbolically associated with the Otherworld. Second, "she brandished a whip with silk lashes and a ruby stock." This accentuates the "goddess of wild beasts" aspect that this character assumes. Cundrie the Sorceress is the representation of an ancient woodland deity, an archaic Artemis from a time when she was not the pleasant pedestrian of Roman mythology but the dreadful whip-wielding solar goddess of the Greeks and Scythians, who was always ready to demand more victims for her altars. Here is one more detail from Wolfram's text that proves the existence of an incontestable Eastern influence.

Cundrie hurls an indictment against Parzival. Insulting him profusely, she speaks to him of his father Gahmuret and his brother Feirefiz and tells him: "One single question asked by you at Munsalvæsche would have earned you more than all the treasures of Taboronit, the pagan city whose queen was won by your brother Feirefiz the Angevin, he who is the black and white son of the sovereign of Zazamanc" (Wilmotte trans., 127–28). This is the first occasion that Parzival has ever heard of his brother. But what is remarkable is that there is absolutely no question of a wound to be healed nor is there any religious context, if the hero had asked the one question he would be rich. That's all. Obviously it remains to be seen what kind of riches Cundrie has in mind. Nevertheless the call is heard. The knights hurl themselves madly into the Quest. Parzival begins his wanderings. The sword he received from the Fisher King breaks. Discouraged he arrives at the dwelling of the hermit Trevrizent who, he will later learn, is his maternal uncle. It is Trevrizent who explains to him—with omissions and lies—some of the Grail's secrets. Among these secrets are some very strange things, especially those items concerning the predecessors of the Grail itself, that Wolfram surely didn't invent.

"When Lucifer with his following made their descent into hell, God replaced him with a Man; he took earth and with it shaped the noble Adam. From Adam's body he detached Eve. Children were born of these two individuals; one of them yielding to immoderation and overween-ing pride defiled his grandmother who was yet virgin. Now many peo-ple, before they understand the sense of these words, are astonished and may well ask how such a thing could occur" (Tonnelat trans., vol. 2, 31). Of course Parzival asks an explanation. The hermit answers: "Adam's mother was the Earth; it was by her fruits that Adam was nourished. In this time the Earth was still virginal. But I did not tell you yet who stole her virginity. Adam was the father of Cain who killed Abel in a trifling dispute. When blood was spilled upon the pure earth it took away her virginity. This virginity was thus stolen by the son of Adam" (Ibid., 32).

First will be noted reference to the tradition, already exploited in the Cistercian Quest, concerning the replacement of the tenth legion of angels (Lucifer and the rebels) by the human race. Next, and this seems particularly important, is the primacy given to the Earth Mother and Virgin. This, according to Wolfram, connects the Grail story to ancient beliefs and rituals of a telluric type of religion. Similar conceptions appear in the pseudo-Map's version of the Quest but in a more veiled form, concerning the Tree of Life that becomes red and sterile when the earth drinks the blood of Abel. In Wolfram's text emphasis is placed on the earth's virginity: Adam fed on its fruits. Therefore, if I am interpreting this symbol correctly, Cain was the first to have exploited the earth by plowing it and sowing it with seeds. This symbolizes the birth of agriculture and the origin of metallurgy as well, since tools are necessary to work the land. The act of plowing the earth is comparable to that of coitus through which a woman is impregnated. This anecdote represents the reversal that took place in the history of humanity, that of the fruit eater transformed into a consumer of vegetables—and animals— hence the beginning of an era of murder and violence. This is the Latin myth of the Golden Age ruled by good King Saturn. This Golden Age came to an end the moment violence appeared. The first men, harvesting fruit, could be labeled as "natural." But they didn't exploit nor try to force this nature. On the contrary they respected it. From the time they started planting they exploited and forced nature to their ends thus setting in motion the process leading to division of labor, social injustice (here is found the thesis put forward by Jean-Jacques Rousseau), and finally industrialized society. The entire history of humanity is here.

Now, when one compares this speech by the hermit Trevrizent with the barren state of the Grail kingdom as depicted in all versions of the Quest, one cannot help but think of this nostalgia for the Golden Age that weighs upon the wounded Fisher King and the castle's inhabitants that is, furthermore, displayed by their tears and grief. Could the real goal of the Quest be the restoration of the Golden Age, that ideal primordial state in which man and nature lived in harmonious balance? We find ourselves here completely in the realm of ecology. And why not? Contemporary ecological hypotheses, even though they are imprecise and unfocused, are grafted upon profound psychological tendencies. And they are not new except to the extent that people have forgotten, in the wake of Marxist as well as liberal theoreticians of the nineteenth century, that nature is not inexhaustible. If necessary one could say that the Grail kingdom, the Waste Land, mirrors certain landscapes of the twentieth century that have become deserts or have been rendered barren through overexploitation, for example by the misuse of chemical fertilizers.

Finally it is obvious that correlations can be made between the Grail Quest and the shamanic quest. Both essentially aim at the reconstitution of the original condition, the primordial state of humanity in which the human being was androgynous (Eve inside of Adam). This androgynous being is not noted in *Parzival* but it is clearly established in the Welsh tale of *Peredur*. In sum, Parzival's mission is essentially shamanic: its objective is the restoration of the original world, or in any event the world before Cain, the symbolic inventor of agriculture and industry.

Trevrizent's long speeches to Parzival are moreover charged with references and reflections in which Neoplatonic and Eastern influences are more than just apparent. The tone is Christian. The themes touched upon are anything but:

> Thoughts can conceal themselves from the rays of the sun, thoughts, though no locks enclose them, remain hidden and impenetrable from all creatures; thoughts are darkness where no light penetrates. But godliness has the power to cast light on all; its rays shine through the walls holding the darkness. (Tonnelat trans., vol. 2)

These statements cannot help but evoke comparison to the very symbol of Buddha whose name signifies the Enlightened (or Awakened— translator's note) One. The human being caged in his thoughts is waiting for a ray of the divine light to awaken him. This human being, while in thought, is a prisoner of *maya*, that is to say, illusion. The divine light causes illusion to disappear and banishes suffering. This is also the stage to which true Cathars should aspire, those who will go from Pure Ones to Perfect Ones.

But Trevrizent goes on to the Grail itself. He reveals to Parzival the identity of the knights guarding the Grail at Munsalvæsche. "They are Templars who are often riding far in quest of adventure. Whatever results from their combats, glory or shame, they accept it with an untroubled heart as payment for their sins." Why the Templars? From a German author one would naturally expect to hear talk of the Teutonic

Knights. Otherwise it is necessary to believe that the mention of the Templars was found in the text of the so-called Kyot the Provencal. But in one sense this choice is justified: at the time in which Wolfram wrote the Templars already had the reputation of constituting a world apart, a veritable state within a state, a sect within the Church. Their pugnacity in combat in the Holy Land, their adroit political sense that led them to establish frequent contacts with the Muslims, their real or supposed wealth, and the marginal nature of their more or less secret ceremonies, which heightened the mystery by which the public regarded them, all of this created a legend. In the beginning of the thirteenth century we haven't yet reached a period of machinations against the Templars such as occurred a century later under Philippe le Bel, but the arguments developed under the instigation of inquisitors and legists in the service of the king of France were already being passed on by word of mouth. What did the Templars do when they were alone? What were their real objectives? What was their true doctrine? As no one could really provide answers to these questions, imagination had to fill the gap.

It is from this perspective, according to Wolfram, that the Templars should be considered as the guardians of the Grail. As they were warriors they could defend the Castle of Munsalvæsche. They could even go far away to fight injustice. And as they were monks and priests as well they were suitable for guarding a spiritual message. It is almost natural to find them at Munsalvæsche. Moreover, Trevrizent tells Parzival how the Grail guardians lead their lives.

Everything that nourishes them comes from a precious stone whose essence is completely pure. If you don't know it I will tell you its name. It is called *lapsit exillis*. By virtue of this stone the phoenix is burnt to ashes, in which he is reborn. It is thanks to this stone that the phoenix molts its feathers to only reappear in all its brilliance, as beautiful as ever. There is no person so sick who, if placed in the presence of this stone, wouldn't escape death for the week following the day on which he saw it. Those who see it cease to age. If they were to be in the presence of the stone for two hundred

years, they would not alter any in appearance save that their hair
would turn white. This stone confers such vigor upon men that
their flesh and bones immediately become young again. This stone
is also called the Grail. (Tonnelat trans., vol. 2, 36)

This is quite explicit. Never before have more details been provided
on the Grail and its capabilities. Of course it is impossible to see a
Christian context in the vibrant description given by Trevrizent.
Everything is pagan. It brings to mind the famous Banquet of
Immortality presided over by the head of Bran the Blessed in the second
branch of the Welsh *Mabinogion*. It is also reminiscent of all the other
Immortality Feasts that can be found in humanity's various religious
traditions. It is a restoration of the Golden Age, as well, since there is no
need to exploit and force nature. The Grail feeds the guests and maintains them in a state of eternal youth. This idea is not specifically
Wolfram's, since other versions describe how the passing of the Holy
Grail furnishes the guests with all they could wish in the way of food
and drink. But in Wolfram's work it is not the "Holy" Grail. This mysterious stone is instead closer to the Philosopher's Stone of the traditional
alchemists, the supreme goal of the Great Work, that is to say, a spiritual and material quest that, starting with a raw primary material, leads
to the manufacture of a purified material that is full of power. This
Philosopher's Stone permits lead to be changed into gold but that is only
one of its functions. It constitutes the perfect knowledge of the secrets
of life, and it is also a "universal medicine" through which it confers a
quasi immortality. The points of resemblance between Wolfram's text
and traditional alchemical treatises are so striking that it must be
accepted that *Parzival's* author deliberately synthesized the Grail legend
with the traditions of the alchemists, which, let me repeat, were particularly hardy and prolific in Germany during that time.

Nevertheless, Wolfram wrote for a Christian audience in a Christian
society. Somewhat frightened by the pagan aspect of what he had just
written he provided it with a protective Christian coloration, which, it's
true, is quite vague. "Every Good Friday (a dove) brings to the stone the

virtue of providing the best food and drink in the world. Heaven has nothing that is more delicious. The stone also procures game of all sorts for its guardians" (Ibid., 37). The dove is obviously reminiscent of the Holy Ghost, but we have seen that the image itself was of Eastern origin. Everything is presented as though Wolfram von Eschenbach wished to provide a slight boost to the Christian doctrine while still respecting the integrity of his sources, sources that were profoundly pagan in nature. The fact that he added the mention of the dove depositing "a host" upon the stone, whereas in Eastern tradition it is a seed, speaks volumes on this passage's ambiguous nature. We then come to the place in Trevrizent's discourse in which he expounds upon the selection and recruitment of the Grail guardians.

> A mysterious inscription appears on the edge of the stone in which the name and lineage of those—men or maidens—who have been summoned to make the glad voyage, is announced. There is no reason to erase the name as it disappears from sight upon being read. The elect are sought from the most diverse array of lands. (Ibid., 37–38)

This is as much as to say that the brotherhood of the Grail Templars is truly a secret society: the guardians of the Grail are chosen by mysterious means. They are truly the elect. What isn't known is the criteria by which they were chosen. But it is incontestable that these words put in the mouth of the hermit Trevrizent have in large part contributed to the making of the Grail into the pivot of a secret society, whose participants—who are called rather than being volunteers—must follow the stages of an equally secret initiation process. This idea can be found again in Wagner's opera. And there are traces of it in the mysterious and sinister group Thule, from the 1920s, that played no small part in the rise and triumph of the Nazi ideology.

In any event the Grail is well guarded: "In this castle a noble brotherhood resides. Those who are part of it have valiantly fought to prevent the approach of men from all lands to the Grail, outside of those who have been summoned by the Munsalvæsche inscription to enter that holy troop" (Ibid., 39). Here is where the Grail's esoteric nature comes into play: none can enter its sanctuary unless chosen by magic. And none can see the maimed and infirm Anfortas there "because he was rich and young, and in his quest for Love did not respect chastity." In short the titular king of the Grail failed to observe the Golden Rule of chastity. It isn't even a question of applying guilt to sexual relations, as is clearly the case in the Cistercian version of the Quest. The text is quite clear on this point: "in his quest for Love." It seems that the Grail knights were supposed to love but only by sublimating their sexuality and not seeking to satisfy it carnally. The resemblance to the various Hindu and Buddhist Tantric doctrines is quite striking: sexual energy is not denied nor made shameful, nor is it brutalized or repressed, it is only transformed into a quest for mystic love on a higher level of access to the divine. Anfortas was stricken because he failed to understand this. But he isn't damned for it and the proof is that when he is later cured by Parzival he becomes young again and picks up where he left off in his interrupted quest for Love. Wagner adroitly transposed this aspect of Anfortas's problem into his opera. The musician-poet approached the adaptation of this theme from the best possible vantage point as he was confronted by his own sexual impotence in the presence of his still young and ardent wife. Of such things are works of art inspired. . . .

Wolfram is the sole author to fully expose the sexual aspect of Anfortas's wound. In the other versions the Fisher King is wounded in the thigh or leg, a delicate euphemism. In the *Quest,* as in the *Didot-Perceval,* this wound is due to a "dolorous stroke," but the context is quite vague about the precise circumstances in which it occurred. However the connotation is apparent throughout: if the Grail kingdom is stricken with sterility or impotence, it is because the king is himself stricken with the same disorders, which amounts to the same thing. In addition, when Perceval, after having been tempted by the female devil in the Cistercian *Quest,* inflicts an intentional wound upon his thigh it is perfectly clear that it is a case of castration or its simulacrum.

Trevrizent takes advantage of this to speak of the lineage of the Grail.

The grandfather Titurel had a son King Frimutel, who died leaving behind several children, Trevrizent himself, a certain Schoysiane, Repanse de Schoye the Grail bearer, Anfortas the Fisher King, and Herzeloyde, Parzival's mother. He then informs Parzival of his mother's death from the grief she suffered at seeing him leave. He also explains the circumstances in which Anfortas was wounded: "The king of the Grail who sought the love of any woman other than she whose name appeared upon the stone is condemned to pay for it by severe suffering. His war cry was 'Love.' In single combat his virile parts were wounded by a poisoned lance" (Ibid., 44). Since that time he has not been able to be healed despite all the cares lavished upon him nor has he been able to die. He will be cured by a knight who comes and asks *the* question. And Trevrizent reveals the name of the woman loved by Anfortas: Orgeluse of Logroys who has since become the wife of Gawan.

But rare are those who enter the castle. One of those who almost succeeded was the king Lähelin. He killed a knight of the Grail and stole his horse, the same steed that would become Gringuljete (the doughty White One), Gawan's mount. Here we come across the name of Lähelin again, he against whom Parzival seeks revenge, and who has committed wrongs against not only Parzival's mother but also against the Grail guardians. Here we fall fully back into the theme of family vengeance (on the maternal side) that the hero of the Quest must achieve.

Trevrizent, before recognizing Parzival as his nephew, also speaks of "the man who remained simple minded," that is Parzival himself, "who entered Munsalvæsche and then left again burdened with a grave sin because he had not asked his host *what ailed him*" (Ibid., 40). The question is thus very different than those it was necessary to ask in other versions of the Quest. Here it is simply asking the Fisher King the cause of his sufferings. There is nothing to be asked about the Grail, either what it is or who it serves. The principal element of Parzival's quest is therefore not so much to discover the Grail—the object has no need of discovery—but to heal the wounded king so that his kingdom will regain its fecundity and equilibrium. This conforms perfectly, moreover, with the archetype of the tale that is visible in *Peredur* and *Jauffré*. The Grail, as mysterious and sacred as it is, remains nonetheless only a secondary element, completely distinct from the aim of the original Quest. The dominant theme is of a blood vengeance that would obtain the healing of the king and the "renewal" of his kingdom.

Now Parzival knows what question he must ask his maternal uncle Anfortas, the Fisher King. Trevrizent then launches into some obscure astrological considerations that are quite unorthodox and spell out, as well, that Anfortas's wound is even more painful when the weather is freezing. He also informs Parzival that Ithier of Gaheviez, the trouble-making knight at King Arthur's court who stole the cup and was killed by the hero, was of the same lineage as themselves and that numerous Grail knights wander throughout the world incognito in order to right wrongs wherever they occur. Parzival makes confession to Trevrizent and leaves to try and bring his mission to an end.

Wolfram next recounts the adventures of Gawan, also a participant in the Quest, adventures that are only further developed versions of those that can be read in Chrétien's work and that of his first continuator. But the famous Orgeluse plays a large role here. First we see Gawan at the Castle of Wonders. Where this episode received cursory treatment at the hands of Chrétien de Troyes, Wolfram provides more detail. The master of the Castle of Wonders is the magician Klingsor, and the description of the castle, as said earlier, brings to mind the description of a Buddhist monastery. Emerging triumphant from the trial of the Bed of the Marvel, Gawan is welcomed and cared for by the ladies of the castle, who are obviously the Flower Maidens from Wagner's *Parsifal.*

Gawan still has numerous adventures to undergo, notably the one at the Perilous Ford. He then learns who the magician Klingsor really is. He was a former duke of Mantua, punished by a king whose wife he had seduced. He has devoted himself to magic in order to avenge himself on other men for the affront he has received. He has thereby successfully imprisoned within his castle a good number of lords and ladies by virtue of powerful spells. But as he has sworn to allow his prisoners to leave if someone passes the tests, he must accede to Gawan's wishes.

An episode in the *Prose Lancelot* corresponds to this one. There the sorcerer is a sorceress, Morgana. Because she had been deserted by her lover Guyomard, Arthur's sister Morgan the Fee enchanted the Vale of No Return* so that any knight who had been faithless to his lady would remain trapped there, prisoner of his delusions and fantasies. Only a knight faithful to his lady could overcome the tests and break the spell. This knight was Lancelot of the Lake, desperately faithful to Guinivere. From that day forward Morgan's hate for Lancelot grew.

There is something ambiguous about Klingsor's story. In short, his magic castle is a fake Munsalvæsche and Klingsor himself is a sort of black and malefic double of Anfortas. In addition his palace is constructed in the style of a Buddhist monastery. I would really like to know where Wolfram von Eschenbach was coming from. And why was King Arthur's mother, as well as Gawan's own mother and sister, among Klingsor's prisoners? Klingsor's appearance, cleverly exposed by Wagner in his opera, is that of Chronos, overcome and punished by his son Zeus and then relegated to some faraway isle or lost castle in the West. His wound is the same as that of Anfortas, but final; he cannot be cured and his sterility and impotence are definitive. He gets his revenge through enchantments. Here we can see the Indian-Buddhist *maya*. And Gawan, whose solar character is never in doubt in any of the Arthurian tales, illuminates the shadowy areas just by appearing in Klingsor's castle, awakens the sleepers, in other words dreamers, rids them of their illusions, and liberates them. In one sense Gawan is a Buddha, and it is evident he holds an important role in the Quest, even for Wolfram, and even if his role is necessarily secondary to Parzival's.

Subsequently Gawan fights an unknown knight who is Parzival. Both finish by recognizing each other and together they journey to Arthur's court. After various adventures Gawan weds the beautiful Orgeluse but Parzival remains sad thinking of Condwiramurs. He leaves the court and meets a knight who has come from the East. They fight. Parzival's

---

* This legend has been localized, groundlessly, in the famous Val sans Retour in the forest of Paimpont-Brocéliande, near the village of Tréhorenteuc (Morbihan) of which the church forms a veritable museum of Merlin, the Round Table, and the Grail.

sword breaks as predicted. The pagan doesn't wish to strike an unarmed foe. At this point he reveals his name: Feirefiz of Anjou and Parzival recognizes him as his half brother. Parzival informs him of their father Gahmuret's death and brings him to Arthur's court where Feirefiz is welcomed with great honor. But now a disguised messenger arrives who is none other than Cundrie the Sorceress. This time, however, she does not insult Parzival, quite the opposite: "An inscription has appeared upon the stone, said she, and it commands that you become king of the Grail. Your wife, Condwiramurs and your son, Loherangrin* are summoned to the castle as well as yourself." She then traces the destiny of Parzival and his lineage, emphasizes the question the hero should ask and starts raving astrologically giving the stars their Arabic names "known to the rich and noble Feirefiz, who all black and white was sitting close to her" (Tonnelat trans., vol. 2, 298–99).

Cundrie's invitation to Parzival is testimony that, in Wolfram's mind, membership in the Grail knighthood was reserved for the initiate. Parzival didn't succeed in his mission during his first visit to Munsalvæsche *because he hadn't yet been expressly designated by the magic stone,* that is to say, because he hadn't yet provided proof of his ability to rule over the kingdom. Now his destiny has been fulfilled. But what's to be said about the presence of the "black and white" Feirefiz who is of Anjou but is also an infidel? It seems that this presence of Feirefiz in *Parzival*—which is not found in any other version of the Quest—was necessary in Wolfram's mind for carrying out in some way the conjunction between Western and Eastern tradition. In fact Feirefiz's presence and participation in the end of the Quest symbolizes the efforts performed by Wolfram von Eschenbach to unite his two sources of fundamentally different origins, Celtic and Oriental. Also, much could be said about Wolfram's insistence upon portraying Feirefiz as both black and white. As a mixed blood of Angevin and Muslim descent he would have had colored skin, that's all. Why then both black and

---

* Wolfram uses the form Loherangrain which is closer to the original, Garin of Lorraine, hero of the chansons de geste from the Doon of Mainz cycle.

white? Probably to symbolize duality finally reconciled, or even the yin and yang of Indo-Buddhist thought. It should not be forgotten that Feirefiz (sometimes Vairefils) means "gray son." Above all he symbolizes the union of two principles that are contradictory in appearance. Then Parzival, accompanied by Feirefiz, follows Cundrie the Sorceress to Munsalvæsche. Anfortas's wounds have become intolerable. Parzival, after having taken a long while to pray asks Anfortas the question: "Good uncle, what is your illness?" Anfortas is immediately cured.

All of this has the air of a miracle. However it is not one. The question that Parzival must ask and that he does ask, after much reflection, is a salvational question in the sense that it obliges Anfortas to shed his guilt. The Fisher King has been overly shamed, both by the sin he committed in the past and by the shameful illness with which he is afflicted. Imagine a man belonging to an age in which sex is a shameful act, being able to assert before everyone: "My balls are wounded," or even "I have the pox"? Now Anfortas, whether he has truly been wounded in his genitals, or stricken by a venereal disease (symbolized by the blow from the lance), can only confess his sin if obliged to respond to a precise question. In sum he undergoes a veritable catharsis under Parzival's guidance. Once the burden of guilt has been lifted Anfortas no longer feels the shame that his real affliction consisted of; he is therefore healed, and, at the same time, definitively pardoned. It can be asked what the Grail has to do with any of this.

However, Anfortas can no longer be king. It is Parzival, his nephew, his sister's son—in accordance with Celtic custom—who is the new master of Munsalvæsche. Parzival welcomes Condwiramurs there and his two sons, Kardeiz and Loherangrin, whom he doesn't yet know. A great feast takes place during the course of which Repanse de Schoye appears bearing the Grail. But Feirefiz who is pagan doesn't see the Grail. On the other hand he does fall in love with Repanse de Schoye. He is baptized the next day, weds Repanse de Schoye, and leaves with her for the East. Wolfram tells us that she will bear his son who will be the famous Prester John. Thus Wolfram, not satisfied with merely linking the Occidental theme of the Grail to Oriental themes, arranges to establish a connection between the Grail and the fabled kingdom of Prester John that was so renowned in the Middle Ages. Once again Wolfram von Eschenbach feeds esoterism and the so-called secret doctrines.

He does even better: he also hooks to the Grail the legend of Loherangrin, the Swan Knight, a very widespread myth in Western European folklore, a myth that is most likely of Nordic or Germanic origin that was then localized to the Brabant and Ardennes regions around the family of Godefroy de Bouillon. Parzival's son Loherangrin also became one of the Grail guardians, upholding the tradition into historical times. What a handsome family tree for Godefroy de Bouillon, himself a hero of the Crusades and, in his own way, a quester for the Grail.

So there we have Wolfram von Eschenbach's *Parzival*. It is a dense, luxuriant work, filled with chatter that often serves no purpose, astrological considerations, and inspired commentaries on Neoplatonistic thought and Eastern traditions. Wolfram's own contribution to this whole epic remains to be determined. It is highly possible that the Oriental elements crammed into Parzival were borrowed from his models but those elements were definitely not borrowed from Chrétien de Troyes. He has certainly retained the original outline of the Quest, that which appears to be the most Celtic, but, through his interpretations, he has modified it considerably. And what is most clearly evident is that he wished to give the story an Eastern flavor. Hence the role of Feirefiz, and especially that latter's departure for the East with Repanse de Schoye. Thus the two elements borrowed from the East are returned to it, and the Grail becomes a large and legendary mystical fresco reconciling two worlds that are fundamentally opposed in appearance.

It remains no less true that the Grail itself occupies a very secondary position in *Parzival*. It seems that the Templars, the guardians of the Grail and keepers of a secret tradition, are much more important. It seems that the initiatory aspect of the Quest outweighs its purely mystical aspect. In fact it is not through an ascetic lifestyle that one attains Munsalvæsche, but through the fact that one has been mysteriously designated by the letters appearing on the Grail/Stone. When one is a guardian of the Grail one is not only a priest but a warrior. Was Wolfram seeking to effect a reconciliation here between *spiritual* man and *natural* man? Without a doubt. He puts these words in Cundrie's mouth when she is speaking to Parzival: "You have conquered the peace of the soul and you have entrusted physical joy with a faithful desire" (allusion to the hero's fidelity to his wife Condwiramurs). But at what price is the harmonization of these two fundamental tendencies of the human being obtained? This is the point at which everything takes an ambiguous and even dangerous turn.

For the elitism that appears in *Parzival* is even more accentuated than in the other versions of the Quest. It is an elitism that calls for the intervention of a magical decision or divine anticipation beforehand. In the Cistercian Quest only Galahad was chosen by such means. All the other participants in the quest took their chances and the Quest itself was not forbidden to anyone. Starting from this notion of an elitist selection of a brotherhood of Templars, priests and warriors who are the holders of a sacred and secret tradition, one can easily see how certain theoreticians have been able to feed their delusions concerning the "pure race," the "chosen people," and other aberrations that have unfortunately instigated wars, massacres, genocides, and "final solutions." It would be laughable if it wasn't pure tragedy, and also if some of our contemporaries, nostalgic for an outdated state of mind, didn't find in Wolfram von Eschenbach's legend of the Grail an additional reason to believe in biological determinism. But such is the fate of any major work. It carries the seeds of numerous children, some of whom won't resemble it in the least.

The Grail is one of the most remarkable enigmas to come out of the entire medieval tradition, attested to by its multiple aspects, so varied and so contradictory to one another dependng on the times in which the Grail authors wrote and the meaning each deemed most suitable for a divine or magical object. Never has a theme like that of the Grail legend so excited the imagination of those who wished to see behind the smoky veil of appearances. Never has a sacred object been so sought after yet simultaneously so dreaded. It is the *object* whose unreal light bathes the night in which millions of men and women in search of a truth find themselves. In short the Grail is the Philosopher's Stone that everyone talks about and no one has seen. Who will thereby find the courage and wisdom needed to enter the dark foliage of the forest of Brocéliande, in search of a castle that guards a wounded and infirm Fisher King who grieves for a world buried in the darkness of the unconscious.

THE ΠΕΑΠίΠG
⊙F THE QUEST

It would seem that there is nothing to the idea of the Grail as an object. All those striving to find it fail to bring their trials to a successful conclusion. Moreover, in the Cistercian version of the Quest, there is nothing mysterious about the Grail. It appears constantly and everyone knows quite well where to find it. However, the knights chosen take months and even years to accomplish what they should. This implies that the Grail matters little and that the essential concern is the Quest itself. Therefore, it is important to ask what the meaning of this quest can be.

It should first of all be made clear that in ancient texts, particularly those transmitting an initiatory message—and all the versions of the Quest fall into this category—there can never be a single solution. The story of the Quest is only an outline onto which each individual must embroider as he or she sees fit. This is how the various authors proceeded, but each reader can do the same and find his or her own motivations, goals, and interpretations therein. It is said repeatedly that no two human beings are alike. Why seek to make the Grail one single object then? Why seek to fit the itinerary represented by the Quest into a single initiatory framework?

The first thing that needs to be emphasized is that the Quest presupposes an action. Something has to happen, it is necessary for someone to take action and restore a hopeless situation. The desolate and barren Grail kingdom represents this hopeless situation that could also concern a group or an individual torn by anguish. An action is imperative. And the impossible must be attempted. The situation presents an invitation to go beyond oneself, to go beyond what goes without saying, in a search that aims at piercing the veil of the clouds of the unknown.

A Corsican tale collected in Porto Vecchio in 1882, *The Deliverance of the Prince*, demonstrates the necessity of the seeker to go beyond his or her usual limits. At the same time it is a good example of the transposition of the Grail Quest, for in this instance it is achieved by a woman rather than a warrior hero. It concerns a young woman, Catarinella, who, when going to hunt for wood on the slopes of Mount Incudine, constantly hears a voice urging her to climb higher. One day she decides to climb to the top of Mount Incudine. She finds herself in a beautiful garden next to a magnificent castle. A gardener welcomes her, leads her into a room filled with statues and tells her that if she cannot accomplish the task he is going to give her, she will die. He points at a statue: "This is the son of a king and you must marry him." Catarinella asks how she can wed an inanimate statue. The gardener responds that she must traverse the world until she has "worn out seven pairs of shoes and three wooden wands, the first from traversing the different kingdoms and the latter from knocking on doors. If you succeed you will wed the prince and all the treasures here will belong to you." The young woman sets off on this adventure, helped by curious characters who give her magical objects. At the end of her wanderings she returns, and restores life to the prince and the other people turned into statues. She marries the prince, of course, and becomes a powerful queen.

The outline of the Grail Quest is quite recognizable in this story. At question is the restoration of life and prosperity to a sleeping kingdom. The sole notable difference is that the sexual roles are reversed as the charge of the Quest falls upon a woman. But the heroine has been mysteriously designated by the voice that invited her to climb higher. The entire meaning of the Quest is here: to surpass one's habitual limitations, to push back the frontiers of the possible, to go to the depths of the unknown, either heaven or hell; what matters, as Baudelaire said, is to find something new there. It is on this condition that the sleeping kingdom can be reawakened. And the end of the Corsican story is quite revelatory; once she has returned to Mount Incudine, Catarinella dips a wooden wand into some water the gardener has handed to her, and touches the statues with it while saying: "Take this water, I give you life." It is a baptismal gesture, of course, but the symbolism is obvious: the water represents femininity and the wand represents masculinity. The act of dipping the wand into the water and then touching the statues with it is a gesture of fecundity. Catarinella thus performs a symbolic act of sexual union, the primal scene as psychoanalysts would say, in order to bring about the new birth. For only woman, as initiator and potential mother, can provide this new birth that is of an affective and sexual, psychological order. Catarinella, having successfully passed the trials to which she was subjected, then becomes queen of the Grail and all the treasures of the Otherworld belong to her. But none of this would have occurred if Catarinella hadn't made the decision *to climb higher.*

Yet setting off on a quest is a perilous adventure. Not all of the audacious who take up the challenge necessarily return from their expeditions that always takes place within the confines of the Otherworld. On a psychoanalytical level, the hero grapples with all the fantasies that *have crossed the border,* that is to say, have sprung from the unconscious and are revealed on the level of waking consciousness. One must be capable of resisting terrifying visions, because we often keep images and thoughts in our unconscious, which not being admissible, take on the appearance of monsters and demons. The essential then is to objectify them, push them away, and fight them. This is why the heroes of the Quest must combat lions or other ferocious beasts, or dragons. To enter the unconscious is one thing. To feel at ease there is something else entirely. Catharsis consists of accepting the fantasies that we harbor in our unconscious after having caused them to emerge. This is why the presence of a therapist is often necessary when the patient "expresses" what he holds within. This is why, in the tale of the Quest, there are from time to time, hermits or mysterious women that guide the heroes and aid them in vanquishing the terrors born from this materialization of fantasies.

In a similar vein it is easy to see the journey of the apprentice shaman in the trials of the Quest, the individual who, under the guidance of a master present either in reality or thought, will be forced to awareness of the dangers he runs every instant of his wandering. There are numerous analogies between the different versions of the quest and the stories of the ecstatic journeys of shamans. The symbolism is often the same, and in the end the goal is similar: the shaman in fact wishes to heal a sufferer from illness by going in search of the patient's soul in the dark depths of the Otherworld. The aim of his intervention is regeneration just as are the actions of the Grail hero. But I don't mean to imply that *The Quest of the Holy Grail* as we know it is a souvenir of shamanism, even if the elements issued from a primal shamanism are obvious in the beliefs and rituals of Celtic druidism. Only the methods and symbolism are parallel. It seems that the Quest is more a pure, truly scientific search than a healing or simple driving away of wicked spirits.

By the same token it is difficult to make the claim that the Quest of the Grail is a description of the alchemical operations of the Great Work. Certainly numerous elements can be considered as alchemical but it is debatable that traditional alchemy was known as far back as the times in which the archetype of the quest story took shape. The fact that the most frequent references to the Philosopher's Art are found in *Peredur*, and a little in Wolfram's version, most compel us to adopt a very prudent attitude. Alchemy is clearly of Mediterranean origin and the Quest is Celtic, most likely Irish. This doesn't mean to imply that the Irish clerics who transcribed both the texts of classical antiquity and the insular Celtic traditions were not abreast of the hermetic doctrines, but alchemy didn't truly begin to take on importance until around 1200 and then in quite a narrow area of the continent. Moreover, it shouldn't be forgotten that the alchemists, when writing their obscure but imagistic texts, made abundant usage of the mythological and symbolic paraphernalia already present in the epic traditions of the West. Peredur's famous trance before the crow drinking blood on the snow comes especially from a purely Celtic poetic image that has been proven to have been used in Ireland well before this time. Coincidence? Perhaps, but one can also speak of a fusion between two currents of hermetic thought. Because, like all the alchemical texts, Celtic texts often have double or triple meanings. The same holds true for all traditional writings.

The meaning of the Quest is therefore not alchemical in its totality, no more than it arises purely from shamanism. The Grail hero is too self-devoted to be manipulated by any sort of mandatory problematic requirements. At the beginning, Peredur-Perceval is a naïf who is made world wise by the course of his adventures. But he has no sense of the quest he is undertaking. His wandering is anarchistic. He never knows where he is going. He never even knows what he wants, if it is truly to return to visit his mother, or to chase after adventure, or to find Blanchefleur again. He is always forgetting about the Grail procession and others have to remind him of it. And he is always straying from his route. One doesn't really get the impression that the original outline of the Quest was constructed upon an inalterable skeleton. In a certain sense it could be said that Peredur-Perceval is a poet above all, a dreamer. And perhaps this is what gives him his strength.

As a dreamer Peredur-Perceval is comparable to the shaman. It is the oneiric universe, above all, that will be the theater of his exploits and not a well-localized real universe. Definitively speaking, everything happens in his mind. This is why one should never take literally the different events that are described in the tales of the Quest.

Thus the theme of blood is more symbolic than real. One can take umbrage when Grail heroes searching in principle for purity, fraternity, and peace, kill numerous enemies and even kill one another. This would be to misunderstand the value of blood. Blood has in fact a very close relationship with the spirit. In certain traditions, Judaism in particular, blood is the vehicle of the soul, hence the necessity for Jews to refrain from eating meat until all the blood has been drained from it. Hence also the different prohibitions concerning the consummation of blood with the intentional goal of appropriating the spirit of an animal or human being. The theme of vampires refers to this idea, since vampires are undead beings who can only survive by absorbing the living blood of their victims. The fact that the severed head seen by Peredur is bathed in blood and the fact that, in the Cistercian Quest, the Grail contains the blood of Christ demonstrates that this belief in blood as a vehicle of the spirit was shared by all the authors of Grail literature. And basically all of this is only to emphasize the spiritual aspect of the Quest for the Grail. It isn't an object that one is seeking, but what this object contains. Something that can only be the spirit.

To find the spirit it is, however, necessary to leave the raw material, and in this context, the reference is alchemical. Indeed every authentic creator takes a departure from disorganized matter and strives to model it, refine it, and make it intelligible—or sensible. The dreamer does no less, since it is known that the mechanisms of dream rest on the interpretation of matter during sleep. This is also what artists and poets do and, of course, what scientific inventors do. All, by taking hold of primal matter, attempt to attain the Philosopher's Stone, without necessarily wishing that this Stone will change their lead into gold. This is why the heroes of the Quest, except for Galahad who is a disembodied creation, are always young men tied to the land, who know only the rudiments of life and have no precise knowledge of what's going on in the world outside, they're just smart enough to hunt for their food. The Grail hero can only be a man like everyone else. It is only by his personal itinerary that he will set himself above the others. But there is nothing to oppose the fact that the others don't perform the same quest, since the hero is only an idealized figure, a meaningful example under whose features each of us can easily see himself.

The problem is that not everyone manages to complete the Quest correctly enough to enjoy its fruits. This is the point at which everything gets muddled. Here is where the mystery comes in. Here is where it is necessary to speak of *recipes*, in other words *secrets*, that don't seem to have been divulged to the common man but have been reserved for an elite. Many are called but few are chosen and when, in the Cistercian

Quest, the three heroes of the Grail are summoned to rejoin the three pieces of the broken magic sword, Bohort only manages to unite one fragment, and Perceval two. Galahad alone restores the sword to its integrity. Thus a hierarchy, if not an elitism, exists here. And this brings up the capital question of initiation.

It is certain that all the versions of the Quest are initiatory tales. They are far from being merely stories recounted for the pleasure of one's listeners, even if these listeners can easily be satisfied with the apparent meaning of stories' content. The era in which the Grail stories were set down is one in which a great debate was taking place, started by the troubadours, between the partisans of the *Trobar Clus* and those of the *Trobar Leu*, that is to say, between the Hermeticists and those who believed in total openness. The virtues of the *Trobar Clus* have been overly exaggerated, as are the hidden meanings to be discovered in certain works that are, by the admission of their authors, intentionally obscure and difficult to penetrate. Certainly an equivalence can be seen between the songs of the troubadours dedicated to a faraway or inaccessible, ever transient or even completely unknown lady, and the tales in which the Grail is also always fleeting and never attained, and, in some cases, not even ever described. But since there is more suspicion of the *Trobar Leu*, that is to say, the Open Art, it is permissible to think that the narrative poems from around 1200 reveal more innuendo and insinuation than the texts called hermetic. The majority of the Arthurian romances are based on real characters who as actualized manifestations of ancient mythological themes can express these themes without being considered heretical or apostate. The pagan substratum here is indeed important, and to bring it out it was necessary to cover it with a Christian varnish to divert the probings of that era's censors. The same was true for the sculptors of the cathedrals who also transmitted messages that were hardly in conformance with Christian orthodoxy. The authors therefore proceeded with images, adventures, and details that appeared insignificant. They have spread *nugae*, to use a Latin term in fashion during that time, that is to say, "frivolities," "fables." Who, in fact, could have still believed in the fairylike wonderland that suffuses the

Arthurian romances? One surely believed in the Devil and his guises, one believed in miracles, but surely not in fairies, at least not in the clerical world in which the different versions of the Quest were elaborated. But across the *nugae*, the outline of the original Quest remained immutable.

It is this outline that each must rediscover in order to attain the Castle of the Grail. For the Grail in itself is visible almost everywhere. The Grail is at everyone's disposal. But holding it in one's hands is not enough to give one the means of using it. Instructions are not inscribed upon the sacred vessel. Only those who have fulfilled the Quest in certain set conditions can know the means of its employ. Herein lies the difficulty: on the one hand the stages of the initiatory quest are presented under a symbolic form, and on the other, the means of using the Grail is a jealously guarded secret.

It has often been said that real "brotherhoods of the Grail" existed. That was true, at least after the different versions of the Quest were set down, but not before. The Quest for the Grail was prompted by the stories of the Grail. And it is very likely that fraternal communities guarding the great secrets of the Grail could exist even today. It is enough to find them and, especially, once they are located, enough to be allowed to enter. In the Irish story *The Battle of Mag Tured*, when the god Lugh, who is a half-breed of Fomor and Tuatha de Danann, wishes to enter the Tuatha Festhall and attend the veritable council of war taking place there, he must supply proof that he has a place among the others present, all-powerful god that he is. The porter refuses to let him enter if he doesn't display his skills. Lugh has to declare that he is a smith, warrior, harpist, poet, historian, magician, doctor, cupbearer, and bronze forger. In short he must certify that he is *Salmidanach*, that is to say, the "Multiple Artisan," and it is by virtue of this that he gains admission to the final test, a game of chess. It is only after winning that game that he is given permission to enter.

This fable, that can also be found in the Welsh tale *Culhwch and Olwen*, in practically the same words, is quite meaningful. The heroes of the Quest don't gain the right to the Grail on the strength of their good looks alone. They must provide proof of their deeds. The quest itself allows the elimination of many of those called who, like Gawain and Lancelot, were prompted by the best intentions in the world. And the quest includes some imponderable elements. It is not always because he is the strongest or the most learned that the hero discovers the path to take. It is through his simple-mindedness that Perceval discovers the Castle of Corbénic. It is often because of a chance event—calculated, it is true, for divine implications are far from being absent here—that the hero is set on the road to wisdom. There are examples in all the folktales that portray a young man who, *by chance*, gains possession of a magical object or secret that will help him in his venture. It was also allegedly by chance that the bard Taliesin swallowed the three drops of wisdom from Keridwen's cauldron. And the great Irish hero Finn Mac Cumail, the king of the Fiana, owes part of his initiation to extremely strange circumstances.

After having shown proof of his martial valor, the young Demne (Deer) earns the name of Finn (handsome, blond, purebred), spends a year with a smith who gives him his daughter and his arms (a double sexual and martial initiation), and goes to learn poetry from a certain Finneces "who was residing by the banks of the Boyne." Now, "for seven years, Finneces had been on the Boyne watching for the salmon of Fec. It had been predicted that if he ate the salmon of Fec, nothing would remain unknown to him. And he found the salmon of Fec. He gave Demne (Finn) the task of preparing it. But the poet forbid him from eating even a single piece of the salmon. After cooking it the young man brought the fish to Finneces:

> 'Did you eat any of the salmon?' asked the poet. 'No,' said the young man, 'but I burnt my thumb while cooking it and I stuck it in my mouth afterward.' 'What is your name, my boy,' the poet asked. 'Demne,' answered the young man. 'Finn is your name, my boy,' Finneces declared, 'and it is you to whom the salmon is destined, and truly you are Finn.' Thereupon the young man ate the salmon. This is what gave Finn his knowledge. (Markale, *L'Épopée celtique d'Irlande*, 145–46)

This episode is certainly not foreign to our topic, quite the contrary. The salmon is a sacred animal in Celtic mythology, and probably of Nordic "Hyperborean" origin like the majority of druidic traditions brought over from the "Isles in the North of the World" by the Tuatha de Danann. The symbolism of the salmon is extremely important. First of all it can live in saltwater as easily as it does in freshwater. Next, and this is a fundamental detail, if it lives the greater part of its life in estuaries, it is capable of returning to the source. In the Welsh tale *Culhwch and Olwen*, the first Arthurian literary work, there appears the oldest salmon in the world who is supposed to know the secrets that no one else knows. Arthur's companions are questioning different animals for the knowledge of where the prisoner Mabon (the Son), son of Modron (Matrona, the Mother Goddess, undoubtedly a prototype of Morgan) is being held, that is to say, the Young Sun held prisoner by the forces of Night. An eagle tells them:

> Once I went in search of food in Llynn Llyw; coming to a lake, I dug my claws into a salmon, thinking it would assure me a good supply of food for a long time; but he dragged me into the depths and it was only through great effort that I was able to get rid of him. I and my kin fervently lurked in the area to try and tear him to pieces, but he sent me messengers to establish an accord between us, and he came in person to deliver fifty harpoons of flesh on his back. If he knows naught of what you seek I know of no one who would. (Loth, vol. 1)

Indeed the salmon tells Arthur's warriors where the prisoner Mabon is to be found. The salmon takes Kay and Bedwyr on its back and brings them to the walls of Caer Lloyw. We have already visited this city, which is Gloucester, in the text of *Peredur*. This is the land of the witches and the name means "City of Light," which is quite surprising considering it is the prison in which the young Sun is being held captive. Following numerous preparations and a diversion performed by Arthur's army, the same Kay and Bedwyr (who are, let me repeat, the oldest companions of the archaic Arthur) climb onto the shoulders of the salmon, make a breech in the prison's walls, and free Mabon.

Whatever one thinks of this story, we are here at the very heart of the Quest for the Holy Grail. All the explanation for the myth can be found here. Modron is thus matron, both words for "maternal." It is the basis of the name for the Marne River. It is also one of the appellations for the Celtic Mother Goddess. In the Welsh legend, Modron is the wife of Uryen Rhegard (a historical figure that has assumed legendary proportions like so many others) and the mother of Owein, also know as Yvain, Chrétien de Troyes's Knight of the Lion. This Modron very often appears in the form of a bird, which brings us back to the Irish Morrigan, goddess of love and war; she too frequently appears as a crow. It must be pointed out that in the later English version of the Arthurian legend, Thomas Malory's *Le Morte d'Arthur*, Uryen's wife is King Arthur's sister, Morgan. It so happens that Modron is called "daughter of Avallach," which brings us back both to one of Robert de Boron's Grail kings and the famous Isle of Avalon, the true paradise of the Celts. Mabon, the "young son" is the Welsh form of Maponios, attested to in Gallo-Roman epigraphs as a cognomen for Apollo. The meaning of Mabon's imprisonment is clear: we are dealing with the young son held captive by dark powers (the witches of Caer Lloyw). This is strangely reminiscent of the Germanic myth of Baldur who, killed at a very young age by an act of treachery, cannot regenerate the world and rid it of the monsters that cause it so much misery. Now it is necessary to free Mabon precisely so he may hunt the devastation-causing boar Twrch Trwyth. This expedition in search of Mabon refers to traditions going back to prehistoric times, as is indicated by the detail of the salmon. It should be compared to the solar worship of the Bronze Age and the famous solar chariots found in Scandinavia, as well as with the universal myth of the barge of the sun held back in the ocean of night on the other side of the world. The character of Mabon reappears in Renaud de Beaujeu's tale *The Handsome Stranger*, under the name Mabonagrain, and also in Chrétien de Troyes's *Erec*, as well as in Ulrich von Zatzikhoven's *Lanzelot*, an earlier version of Lancelot, under the name of

Mabuz, son of the Lady of the Lake, that is to say, Vivian, and in this last text Mabuz is the prisoner of a spell that Lancelot must break in order to free him.

This speaks of the primary importance of the story of Mabon. It is the deliverance of the Sun prisoner of Night. Is this not what Peredur-Perceval accomplishes in fulfilling his quest? But this deliverance of Mabon can only be obtained by virtue of the salmon. This salmon is not only a provider of knowledge, he is also a provider of food. And this brings to mind the legendary life of Korentin, bishop of Quimper. In his hermitage he fed himself from a salmon from which he cut a piece each day and which on the morrow was as fresh and whole as before. It also reminds one of the early Christian symbol of the fish that represented Christ himself. It must also be remembered that in *The Story of the Holy Grail* by Robert de Boron, the Grail meal took place not only in the presence of the sacred vessel, but also with a fish.

In brief, the initiation by chance of Finn Mac Cumail is due to a salmon. It is this salmon that provides knowledge. The salmon belongs to the oldest layer of Celtic mythology, along with the swan, the animal appearance in the guise of which the fairy beings most often appear. And the guardian of the Grail is the Fisher King.

It is known that Robert de Boron made Bron a Fisher King because he portrayed that individual fishing for a fish to assure nourishment for the community. This is an *a posteriori* explanation that doesn't hold up. Robert de Boron didn't understand the meaning of the myth he was adapting for a later audience and wanted to provide a logical explanation for a title he had necessarily found in his sources, which also constitutes a proof of the ancient nature of the denomination of the Fisher King. The exegetes of the Cistercian Quest spoke of the Fisher King's similarity to Christ. Like Jesus, the Fisher King fished for souls in order to save them. This explanation doesn't hold up either, given the antecedence of the myth and its roots in druidic paganism. In other versions of the Quest the explanation is even simpler: the role of the king is to hunt when he is not making war, but since the Fisher King is wounded, he can no longer hunt and must content himself with fishing to pass the time.

There is no need to refute this explanation. No one has dared venture another: it being a given that the authors of the Arthurian romances like all the authors of the twelfth and thirteenth centuries stuffed their tales with word games, the Fisher King, is in reality the Sinner King,* since he has committed a sin, whether by seeking to look inside the Grail, or by having shameful relations with a woman not worthy of him. However, this explanation should not be overlooked.

It is actually something else entirely. In the fourth branch of the Welsh *Mabinogion* there is an aged king who is the uncle of the magician Gwydion of Gwynedd and a magician himself, and who bears the name of Math, a name that undoubtedly refers to the bear (Arto or Matu), like Arthur. Now this Math has one defect: he is fit in times of war, but in times of peace he cannot live unless his feet are constantly resting in the lap of a young virgin girl. The similarity between the Fisher King and his daughter, the Grail bearer, on the one hand, and Math the Magician King, on the other, is obvious. All the more so when one realizes that the Fisher King could take on any form that he wished. In addition Math is the owner of a magic wand, the phallic significance of which will escape no one. It is also very well known that in psychoanalysis the identification of the penis with the fish is a certainty. There is ample room for speculation here.

The Fisher King is the master of the fish, the Salmon of Knowledge and Abundance. This is his most ancient role in Celtic mythology and all the later explanations can't change a whit of this fundamental aspect of the character. The fish is, symbolically, the most archaic of creatures, since all living things derive from the mutation of a primordial aquatic entity that lived in the vast oceans of the world's beginning. The Welsh text of *Culhwch and Olwen* made it the oldest animal in the entire world, the one who consequently knows all mysteries and secrets. In Germanic mythology, Loki, the troublemaker, but also the prompter of the world's mutations, transforms himself into a salmon. In the Finnish (thus

---

* The wordplay here doesn't translate into English. In French the Fisher King is the Roi-Pêcheur and the Sinner King is the Roi-Pécheur—translator's note.

Finno-Ugrien) in which shamanism played a large role, this salmon is of great importance. In the Finnish *Kalevala* we indeed see the primordial bard Vaïnämoïnen discovering the divine spark inside a pike that had swallowed a salmon. Moreover, among certain Amerindian peoples, whose traditions have issued from Asiatic and northern European shamanism, it is told how Fire is in the possession of the chief of salmons. And what is to be said concerning the countless folktales in which a fish caught by a fisherman saves its life by bestowing wealth and inviolability upon the latter on condition that he releases it?

The key to the Grail Quest is in this initiation of Finn that is due to the salmon of Fec. The salmon of Fec is indeed the same fished for by the Fisher King, and who he releases on the promise of receiving the infinite riches of the Otherworld. Where is the Grail holding the blood of Christ in all of this? Not so far away since all myths have this distinguishing feature, they survive under different colorations and ideologies. The Christian message is not in contradiction with the message of the quest archetype. The blood of Christ is a food for the same reasons as the flesh of the salmon given to the eagle, for the same reasons as the salmon of Fec ingested by Finn Mac Cumail, and for the same reasons as the fish allegedly caught by Bron. There is no gap between the different sources of the Grail Quest. There cannot be any in the Quest itself since it is the result of a synthesis masterfully accomplished by the various authors from the end of the twelfth and beginning of the thirteenth centuries.

The most important thing to know is what is truly concealed under the symbol of the salmon. This knowledge is without a doubt more important than the knowledge of what is contained within the Grail object. We have said it could just as easily hold the blood of Christ as a severed head, a host, or the heart and sexual organ of a lover who is victim (host) of the jealousy of a dozen cuckolded husbands, for the greatest ecstasy of a dozen young women madly in mystical love. Everything is connected and is held together in the domain of mythology. In truth, the Grail can contain anything, in other words all or nothing. Why couldn't it hold the salmon?

In fact, this mythic salmon represents the primordial individual. Hence the true object, within the context of the Quest, is the rediscovery and embodiment of this individual in the final stage of a long personal experience. Two exemplary stories from Irish epic literature will help us understand.

The Inundation of Loch Neagh is the Gaelic version of the legend of the Town of Ys, in which a catastrophe destroys the town and swallows it beneath the waters of a fountain. The person responsible for this tragedy, a certain Libana, like the Dahud of the Breton legend, lives in the depths, first in a chamber that has a strong resemblance to a womb. Then, as she grows bored, she starts praying and transforms into a salmon: "Only her face and breasts remained unchanged." Then she swims in the waters of the lake for three hundred years before being caught by Saint Congall. This latter individual baptizes her under the name of Muirgen (Morgan), that is to say, "Born of the Sea," but Libana-Muirgen dies at the moment she receives her baptism.

This first tale, in short, gives us the original Woman, she who lives beneath the waters, analogous to the virgin Ilmater of the Finnish *Kalevala*. She is the Mary-Morgan of countless folktales, who dwells beneath the threshold of the unconscious and only reveals herself on certain occasions. She is mistress of the mysterious domain that lies in the aquatic depths, where she has a room or a luxurious palace like the Lady of the Lake from the Arthurian romances. A deity of the waters, of course, but also the mother of humankind. In the Irish tale, which bears the mark of an excessive Christianization, she cannot survive her baptism because with that she has completely fulfilled her mission, the tradition she represents has been totally absorbed into the Christian doctrine.

The second story is a strange text concerning a certain Tuan Mac Carill. This personage supposedly lived numerous lives and was the privileged witness of all the real and mythical invasions that took place in Ireland since the dawn of time. He crossed through the centuries in different shapes. He was first a man, then a stag, then a boar, then a vulture during the epoch in which the sons of Milhead, that is to say, the

Gaels, invaded the Emerald Isle and vanquished the Tuatha de Danann.

> Sleep weighed heavy on me for the space of nine days. I was
> changed into a salmon. Then I found myself in the river. I was well,
> I was fit and happy. I knew how to swim well and I long escaped all
> dangers, the hands of the fishermen armed with nets, the talons of
> the vultures and the spears that fishermen hurled at me. But a fish-
> erman caught me and took me to the wife of Carill, king of this
> land. I have a very vivid memory of this. The man put me on the
> grill. The woman ate me all up. I remember the time when I was in
> the belly of Carill's wife. I also remember that after that I began to
> speak like men. I knew all that had been in Ireland. I was a prophet
> and I was given a name. I was called Tuan, son of Carill. (Markale,
> *L'Épopée celtique d'Irlande*, 21–25)

Cases of fertilization through the mouth are not rare in Celtic
mythology and the example of Taliesin, ingested in the form of a grain
of wheat by the goddess Keridwen to then be recreated by her in the
form of a child that knows all and is endowed with magical powers, is
the best known. In this context the Tuan Mac Carill story cannot help
but bring to mind the identification between fish and penis. The real
meaning of the tale concerning Tuan Mac Carill is quite clear. The wife
of Carill joins sexually with the primordial fish caught by her husband
and gives birth to a prophet who has all the knowledge in the world. It
is obvious that Carill is the Fisher King, wounded and impotent, who
provides his wife, symbolizing the kingdom here, with the fertilizing element that has been lacking for the kingdom's survival. We are thus fully
within the framework of the Grail Quest.

This shows us that the sexual component cannot be overlooked in the
case of the Grail. But this component is not clad in the guise of a banal
eroticism: it concerns a desperately awaited fertilization so that the kingdom can regain its life and prosperity. The salmon is therefore the Young
Son, he who is destined to fulfill the last stage of the Quest. Tuan Mac
Carill, through his numerous existences and experiences, proved he was

the best at realizing the primordial man within himself. It is for this reason that he was selected—caught through fishing—and devoured by
woman. It can also be seen, incidentally, that the man-eating component is portrayed in this aspect of the quest as well.

All of these developments on the salmon, symbol of Knowledge and
man in the integrity of his being, show us that Finn, by ingesting the
salmon of Fec, though it was originally destined for the poet Finneces,
has attained a high degree of initiation: and in the end this initiation
doesn't amount to much, just a sudden grasp of the primordial unity of
being. But it is because he has had this revelation that Finn is endowed
with certain powers of divination and regeneration. Perceval, or
Peredur, has acquired this awareness at the end of his quest. Galahad as
well, and this explains his mystic trance when he discovers what is inside
the Grail. *He discovered nothing other than himself,* but a total "himself,"
that is no longer rent by illusionary contradictions.

This is the meaning of the Quest for the Grail. This quest, marked by
widely varying events that represent so many stages of reflection, leads
he who fulfills it to pierce the screen of illusions that prevent the mind
from distinguishing the Real from the True. For the true is only a game
of the mind where one can cheat at will; truth is only the transposed
image of that which lies beyond, but reality is something else entirely.

In the philosophical system of the Celts there is no fundamental
opposition between opposites. Life and death are only two aspects of
one unified reality. Body and mind are also two aspects of one reality,
that of existence, but not from a materialist perspective. It is not the body
that gives rise to the mind, which would be a return, in an inverted
fashion, to the spiritualist dogma that the mind gives rise to the body,
and it is known that neither assertion is demonstrable. All Celtic texts or
those inspired by them seem to proclaim this assertion through the
symbolic adventures of heroes fallen from heaven. In fact, the heroes are
men like any others, and the only gods are those that are embodied
aspects of the Superior Beings' divine functions. There has never been
any antimony between the druidic doctrine and the evangelical message, hence the easy recuperation of the Grail myth by Christianity. The

Grail seen by Galahad is the same one seen by Peredur, and yet they are not the same. Let us recall that it is always the same river but never the same water that is flowing under a bridge, and that the paths that ascend are also those that descend. This Heraclitian thinking, previous to the Greek miracle, is also "barbarian" thinking. It is that of the Celts.

It remains no less true that the Grail, buried in the Castle of Corbénic, mocks all those who set off in search of it. Is it up too high? Is it down too far, buried in the caverns of the earth, where sleeping dragons lie ready to wake up and devour the audacious individual who enters? It seems that the Grail is neither too high nor too low, and that the solution is much simpler. A widespread folktale, but of which a very concise version can be found in the Sufi tradition, gives it to us. An inhabitant of Baghdad dreams that a treasure is hidden at a certain spot in the city of Cairo. He reaches Cairo toward the end of the story and is arrested there as a thief. He manages to vindicate himself to the police lieutenant and recounts his dream to him. The other man then tells him that he had dreamed the same thing: a treasure hidden in such and such a house on such and such a street in Baghdad. The man from Baghdad sees that it is his own house the lieutenant is speaking of and returns home to discover the treasure.* This theme has often been exploited in comic works but it is nevertheless extremely serious. When one wishes to find something, it is necessary to leave home, for when one is too close to something, one pays it no mind, and most importantly, doesn't perceive its real value. To discover the real it is first of all necessary to escape this real in order to examine it retrospectively. Countless stories from the universal tradition show us poor men sleeping on top of a treasure they are incapable of seeing. By the same token, when the hero of the Quest finds himself in the castle of the Grail, *he doesn't know what it is*, at least not during the first visit. He has not yet looked around himself enough to discern the multiplicity of the Being and understand that this multiplicity merges together into a fundamental unity. He thus sees nothing. In the same way numerous knights who have set off on the

*Eva de Vitray Meyerovitch, *Les Chemins de la Lumière* (Paris: Éditions Retz, 1982), 129.

quest pass by the Castle of the Grail without seeing it. Without even seeing that there is a castle. For the door of the castle is always on the inside. It is the open door to the closed palace of the king.

The wisdom attained by the winner of the Quest is within the reach of everyone. But as is most excellently said by the Trouvère* Thibaud de Champagne, "the messengers are illuminated by night, and during the day they remain invisible to folk." Everything is symbol. Everything is language. We must take risks and burrow into the Night, for it alone can show us the path. This is the reason the visionary sages, philosophers, and saints are often portrayed as blind men. The Sun of the Night is not the same as that which shines during the day, but its brightness is much more dazzling, and it permits the human spirit to be a druid in the etymological sense of the word, that is to say, "far seeing."

One will therefore see all the inevitable consequences that arise from this Quest for the Grail. It represents a supreme moment in human thought, one of those privileged moments in which the landscape, illumined by a marvelous light, shows up clearly on the horizon. And in this landscape the Grail is hiding. It is up to us to awaken what it contains.

* A Trouvère is a minstrel of Northern France—translator's note.

ÍNDEX